On Choreography & Making Dance Theatre

Mark Bruce has choreographed, directed and danced internationally for nearly thirty years, working with Rosas, Bern Ballet, Ballet Black, Introdans, Gibson / Martelli, Probe, and DJazzex among others.

He formed the Mark Bruce Company in 1991. Productions include *Moonlight Drive* (1991), *Lovesick* (1995), *Helen, Angel* (1996), the celebrated collaboration with Polly Jean Harvey and John Parish *Dance Hall At Louse Point* (1997), *Horse, Dive* (1999), *Sea of Bones* (2006) *Love and War* (2010), *Made in Heaven* (2012), *Dracula* (2013) which won the Sky Arts South Bank award for Dance, the National Dance Award for Best Male Dancer for Jonathan Goddard as Dracula, and the award for Best Independent Company, *The Odyssey* (2016), and most recently *Macbeth* (2018).

Bruce's theatre work includes the Royal Exchange Theatre's productions of *The Bacchae, Antigone, The Glass Menagerie, The Revenger's Tragedy, Antony & Cleopatra, Peer Gynt, As You Like It, Fast Food, Still Time* and *The Way of the World*. He co-devised *Skellig*, an opera based on the book by David Almond, for the Sage Gateshead in 2008. He directed Rick Bland's award winning *Thick* which toured the UK, US and Canada. Bruce also worked with Singapore Repertory Theatre on their 2015 production of *The Tempest*. He has worked in a variety of new media, screen and interactive stage productions with Gibson / Martelli.

In 2005 Bruce choreographed *Fever to Tell* for Probe, *Green Apples* for the Royal Opera House's Clore Studio Summer Collection and *Bad History* for The Place Prize 2006. In 2008 he created *The Sky or a Bird* for Probe's 2008 UK tour and *Stars* for Dance South West. Bruce's first commission by Bern Ballet, *Crimes of Passion*, premiered in January 2010 and his second, *Medea*, in February 2011. He created *Second Coming* for Ballet Black in 2015.

BlackBirdRedRose Studios was established in 2017, a base for Mark Bruce Company to create, rehearse and film its productions and run education programmes, including its international summer school. Mark was also on the Contemporary Category Final judging panel for BBC Young Dancer 2017.

Mark writes music for his own work, published by Mute Song.

MARK BRUCE

On Choreography & Making Dance Theatre

OBERON BOOKS
LONDON

WWW.OBERONBOOKS.COM

First published in 2018 by Oberon Books Ltd
521 Caledonian Road, London N7 9RH
Tel: +44 (0) 20 7607 3637 / Fax: +44 (0) 20 7607 3629
e-mail: info@oberonbooks.com
www.oberonbooks.com

A catalogue record for this book is available from the British Library.

PB ISBN: 9781783197774
E ISBN: 9781783197781

Cover image by Nicole Guarino

Printed and bound by 4EDGE Limited, Hockley, Essex, UK.
eBook conversion by Lapiz Digital Services, India.

Contents

Note

You will notice that, apart from crediting in photographs, I don't refer to any of the artists I have worked with by name. Those I have worked with will know I am talking about them. If you would like to know more about these wonderful people it is relatively easy to find out who they are and more about them. You could start at: markbrucecompany.com, where you will also find video footage of some of the work mentioned in this book.

Introduction

There is no definitive method of choreography. Any choreographer who has a voice has found and executed it in their way. Choreographers pick up things here and there from what they experience, what they see, who they work with, and assemble a craft themselves. When I was training to be a dancer choreography was barely on the curriculum, but we were enabled to make work and perform it. If you wanted to do this you got it together and worked at it yourself.

So much of what we do as artists is intuition and instinct. The process of creativity often resides in chaos, cannot be tamed, fully understood or concluded. We are dealing with imagination. Magic. It is like trying to rationalise the Dionysian – the mysteries, the savage, the beauty and the madness. My aim as an artist is to tap the subconscious, our hearts; transcend our everyday lives and hopefully stumble upon some truth along the way.

However, it isn't that easy. True, we don't have to completely understand why we make a work, or all of what it is about, or how we put it together. Most dancers will have one good piece of expression in them without having a clue how they did it. But when things calm down and you've made a certain amount of work, if you are going to develop, move forward, at some point you will need to understand more about what it is you do. You will have to step back and start understanding and learning your craft so you can improve and develop it, and that is indelibly connected with understanding more of what your work is about.

This book is about a craft that I am still learning and evolving. But this is only how I do it and I don't have one fixed method. Others will work differently, and there is no right or wrong way. My work, if it has to be labeled, is 'dance theatre'; therefore its dramatic content is inextricably linked with movement, and in writing about my methods I cannot completely separate the two. If you are convinced your interest lies only in the abstract, this may not be the book for you. But then again it might, if it enables you through rejection to clarify your approach.

I want this book to be of practical use. I have choreographed for many years and there are all sorts of things one needs to be aware of, prepared for, when setting out to translate the beginnings of an idea in one's mind into a finished full-length piece of work that will be shown to the outside world. Because – believe me – there are all sorts of forces, from outside and within, that can destroy that little gem you are cradling inside you.

Choreography

Choreography is the creation and composition of movement or dance. (You can find any version of this statement in a dictionary.) A choreographer is an artist whose means of expression is movement. Whether to touch a viewer emotionally, challenge, entertain, tell a story, a concept – whatever they want; a professional choreographer should have the skill to open a viewer's subconscious and communicate using movement as their primary tool. But to be a choreographer you can't just be good at creating movement and putting it together. There are many other skills and knowledge one needs to produce a piece of work. If I was to describe the basic foundation or ingredients of my version of dance theatre I would state: Movement, drama, sound and vision. You can spend your whole life studying just one of these crafts. A choreographer has to study all of them to the best of their ability and learn how to combine them.

Leonard Cohen wrote of 'The Tower of Song'. In my mind this tower, lonely as it is, is full of a thousand great songwriters. The tower of literature must be heaving with great writers, the tower of painting, theatre, music, film… but the tower of choreography? In my mind this would be a lonely place.

Dance is a powerful art form. Like music, it can communicate beyond words. It is ritual. It is animal. It is ancient and universal and has been around since man first started to draw on cave walls; maybe even before. But once you remove traditional dance, why is the art form of choreography so young? 'Modern dance' was only officially invented in the last century whereas literature has evolved since it was invented. Look at the journey of music. The wealth and range – you can't begin to fathom it. Film, only possible within the last hundred years or so has grown, despite the great expense and logistics of producing it, and there are thousands of groundbreaking films out there, many great film makers, and any number of books written about how sophisticated and diverse the methods of producing it are.

How many books are written about choreography compared to those written about other art forms? How many 'experts' on choreography are there? Make a list of great choreographers, then write another of great writers. The writers' list is going to go on and on and back through the centuries. You could spend your whole life reading great writers and only scratch the surface of what is out there. But I suspect your great choreographers list will run dry pretty soon and all will be within the last hundred years.

There *are* great choreographers. But not thousands of them. Choreography is an obscure and rare talent. Knowledge, experience and craft can produce better, even good, choreographers. But real talent, that 'something else', I suspect one is born with.

There are many skills needed to become a professional choreographer, and they don't always sit well together. I will write about the skills I need as I go through the process of making a dance work from scratch, and highlight how, despite making work for several decades, I feel I have so much more to learn.

But something to think of:

Muhammad Ali had the two basic prerequisites to becoming a choreographer. He had a keen mind, but he had the talent and discipline to put his mind to rest and dedicate himself to the laborious rigours of physical training he needed to become a skilful, creative and powerful animal able to step into the ring and beat the crap out of anyone, and dance as he did it. In short, he could compete in two rings – that of the mind and that of the body.

Ideas

One of the most common questions students ask about work is: 'Where did it start?' or 'What was your inspiration?' and the inevitable: 'Where do you get your ideas from?'

If asked to identify the true starting point of any work I'd have to say 'I don't remember'. A piece begins with a collection of interconnected ideas – images, feelings, movement, music, dreams – anything – things that are special to you. But the origins, or beginnings, of ideas are obscure.

Imagine a pool of water, deep and dark – you can't see or touch the bottom. This pool is your subconscious, and at times bubbles ripple up to the surface where they pop. And there they are: 'ideas'. Something in the depths of that pool has sent them up to your consciousness. Your consciousness becoming aware of an idea is often what one refers to as the beginning inspiration of a work. But if one was to find a true beginning of an idea you would have to dive to the bottom of that dark pool to find the origins of those bubbles. We are a product of our ancestry, our genes, the world around us. Our ideas begin before we are even born. What makes them suddenly open in your mind is another thing. I may say an idea came from a moment in the studio, or listening to a piece of music, reading a particular passage in a book; but these would only be what triggered something much deeper inside me. And that is why we can't truly *remember* where our ideas start. If you ever reach the bottom of that dark pool you'll be the first. You may also stumble upon the meaning of life while you're down there.

The next question often asked is: 'How do you get ideas?'

You can gain experience, learn craft, technique, tricks, all kinds of tools to enable you to make your work. But one has ultimately little control over whether ideas come to you or not. I am rubbish at maths, science, languages; I can't fix cars or do DIY, I can't build anything, I don't work with electrics or plumbing. I can't spell. I forget things. I love history but I can't remember dates. This list could go on and on – I often feel there are whole sections of my brain missing because of my lack of ability to do or understand certain things. But I have an imagination that produces ideas. I have them every day. I carry a notebook with me at all times so I can write them down. Sometimes I can listen to a piece of music once and I've already created a dance piece in my head. My ideas aren't necessarily all good, and many of them get lost because I can't read my writing when I go back to them, and many I throw away. I have notebooks everywhere. I don't know what to do with them all. Recently I considered burning a load of them. If I can't find my pen (which is often) I start freaking out. I get visual ideas, narrative ideas, characters come and talk to me in my head, I get movement ideas – technical, or as a form of emotional expression, symbolism, storytelling. I hear music in my head. I feel pace, timing, phrasing that will capture something inside of people. I have ideas of how to develop and sew a collection of ideas together, where to place people in space. I see what colours I want to use. I see sets, costume. I feel atmospheres, locations and have ideas of how to create these for an audience.

It is strange to earn a living from my imagination because I am reliant on something I have relatively little control over, and I often feel I am a vessel for some creature inside me that may or may not turn up to work, and when it does, scatters its notes all over the floor and expects me to sort it all out. All this does not mean I am special or unique. It is just the way I am. We are all meant to do different things; this is the way the world goes round. If I didn't have this imagination, these ideas I wouldn't attempt to do what I do, no matter how desperate I was to do it.

If you do have ideas, and feel there are more ideas to come; stimulate your imagination by stimulating your mind and body. Everything you soak up in life will feed your imagination and the most seemingly unlikely things can get your creativity working. But I would advise not to feed yourself on too much mental junk food. Junk is part of life. I watch low-budget horror films sometimes and I think they influence my work in an interesting way. There is something profound in everything – even trash – because it is all part of what we are. But I feed myself on other things too. So much is instant nowadays and there is a push to make this a prime ambition. We are reduced to snap one-line answers, so much of what we deal with is superficial and we are distracted and desensitised by overstimulation. This can counteract our imagination. We used to have to engage our imagination more, picture what wasn't given to us and therefore exercise the mind. That's what old *Doctor Who* series did for a whole generation. It's how a good book works. It's what you do when you are bored – rather than play with a smart phone. Social media has also enabled us to avoid being alone. We can be virtually with someone at all times. But being alone is important, essential if you want to create. We need time to see, absorb and look further into ourselves.

When I was a teenager you saved up and bought a record. You took it home and listened to every track, carefully turning the sides over. The only other thing you had was the record cover which you would study, imagining what this band was like or who an artist was. David Bowie opened our subconscious by giving us so much, but leaving us in the mysteries – asking us to put it together ourselves; enter our individual subconscious. I remember waiting up till 2 a.m. to watch the film of the Monterey Festival on TV because Jimi Hendrix was on it and I was desperate to see him play. Now you can watch a thousand films of him instantly on YouTube. Of course this is great, but some mystery has been lost; everything is given, and given fast, so we don't have to think. This can make us feel as artists that there is a rush to get things out, produce work fast, just to keep up. It is important to work against this mentality because it is not set up to breed good, strong ideas.

We are, and must be, a product of our time but sometimes it's good to search out the dull dusty stuff on the shelves that's always been there. If it's still there, there might be a reason. Look at here and now but also look back. There are great things in front of you that, given time, will burrow themselves into your psyche and connect with things of depth inside of you.

For years ideas emerging in my work have found parallels with ancient Greek mythology and Tragedy. Finding these connections has added perspective and understanding of what I am doing, they have stimulated other ideas that have enhanced and developed my work. The homecoming of Dionysus in Euripides' *Bacchae* has always resonated with me; how Euripides handled his story, his characters, philosophy; his capturing of 'otherness', what he was exploring. The demigod Dionysus, the maenads – I had equivalent creatures in my imagination long before I read this play that was written around 405BC. How artists have developed themes and ideas over the centuries gives one courage to do the same – just connecting Greek mythology to Ovid to Shakespeare is enough to open a whole load of doors to the imagination. Or a more recent example in a shorter timeframe: H. G. Wells' *When the Sleeper Wakes*, George Orwell's *1984*, David Bowie's *Diamond Dogs*. When we are young we think our ideas are new. You may well have the beginnings of a voice that is unique and relevant to your time but versions of your ideas will very likely have been pursued before because we are all human and dealing with the same things. And when I say study that doesn't mean write and map everything down, just experience it. Soak it up. If it resonates with you it will tap your subconscious, a seed will be planted and it will do its job. Movies I saw when I was young – I didn't study them, I just watched them and they snaked their way inside me and met with other things along the way.

MOVEMENT IDEAS

Of course ideas transgress art mediums – this is what I spend most of my time exploring and is fundamental in how I form my version of dance theatre. It's why I formed a company, so I could embark on the long journey of connecting everything that influences me, all my ideas, and combine them in a way that is mine and communicates with an audience. But – is choreography the best way to express your ideas? Do you have a complex concept for a piece but no ideas for translating this to movement? Do you actually have movement ideas? Is there a better medium suited to express your particular ideas? These may seem obvious things to ask, but before you embark on a journey with choreography it may be good to stand back and honestly answer yourself these questions. If your ideas may be heading for a basis in another art medium – this is going to require a whole other path of learning. I remember an interview with John Lee Hooker in which he was asked if he had any advice for those budding musicians out there and he said something like 'Ask yourself honestly if you are talented at it. If you are, put in the hours and work hard at being the best you can be.'

Choreographers work in many different ways. I am what one might call a traditional choreographer – as in I create my own movement material and I have never stopped physically working at this – exploring, pushing myself to extend and develop movement vocabulary that is individual to me, relates to who I am, how I want to express myself in the medium. And to do this I need tools – technique to stimulate, understand, develop, and enhance ideas and communicate them to those I am working with. However you end up making work, I believe if you want to choreograph you should, if you can, train as a dancer. You may not be the best dancer in the world but you should strive to gain as much physical knowledge and varied technique as you can. And once you have trained you should try to get a job as a dancer and work with as many different choreographers and fellow dancers as possible and not just restrict yourself to staying in your home country. Learn technique and then go through the process of trying to release it, something one will never completely achieve. Be patient – you don't just graduate from dance college as a choreographer. Of course you can choreograph as soon as you want – I started as soon as I began training, but get out there and experience as much dance as you can. It will fuel your array of movement ideas and vocabulary. I had a career as a dancer, so I know how many things I wouldn't know about movement if I hadn't done all those years of physical work and learnt from the great artists I had the privilege of dancing alongside.

Unfortunately dance training is laborious and painful and involves years of mind-numbing repetition. This is because the body grows and develops at a slower rate to the mind and it takes a real determination see it through. There are years of frustration when you feel you are not getting anywhere, in fact sometimes it seems you are going backwards. It can turn you into a kind of stubborn workhorse, a creature that doesn't think, just gets its head down and pushes on; which in many ways is no bad thing. Life as a professional dancer is ruthless; either you are going to make the grade or not. You are working on the animal, the physical being that is going to have the technique and power to express itself through movement. There is something savage in this. And this is good. I want to know the creature inside me so I can unleash it. But the animal of the dancer can get trapped in a mentality of working without thinking. It can begin to stop feeding the mind. The mind can get left behind, and an insular existence can form, which will not always help stimulate ideas. So we have a catch-22 to work against. As I said in my introduction – having ideas for movement is not enough. You need to stimulate your mind outside of this bubble. That's not saying you can't make just pure dance pieces. But there are many 'pure' dance pieces out there that would benefit from knowledge of the world outside of dance and of other art forms. So you need to be disciplined in both mind and body.

We all see differently depending on what it is we do. A graphic artist will see what is before them – form, structure, shadow; a myriad of things because their job involves picking up a pen or pencil and recreating it. Open a car bonnet – I'll see a vague machine; a mechanic will see something different, components they understand; a system. An architect looking at a building will be able to see how it was designed, the materials it was built with, and its relation to the history of architecture. A choreographer must open their eyes to many things but primarily all movement around them. Everything that moves has accents, a style, pace, phrasing that communicates its nature. Animals are an obvious and excellent example of this, but see everything that moves, from a tree in the wind to a subway train hurtling into a station. And hear the sounds that go with that movement. See how movement has been enhanced in movies and listen to the sound that is put with it. Watch Vladimir Horrovitz's fingers moving across the keyboard, or the way Johnny Winter, Buddy Guy or Jimi Hendrix work the fret board and associate this with the unique sound they produce. A great choreographer can take the most basic of steps, a vocabulary we all know, yet create magic from them just by the way they demand a phrase is executed and its relationship to music.

Listen to different music. Some will elicit no response, but change the track and suddenly there is movement brewing inside you. Watch dance that you are drawn to and admire. Look at traditional dance and recognise its birth with a particular response to a type of music connected with a particular culture. Again, you should study as much technique as you can, but also just watch good dance. It will get inside you. Think of the dance numbers of Gene Kelly, Debbie Reynolds, Donald O'Connor and Cyd Charisse in *Singin' in the Rain*, or incredible sections from *West Side Story*, or Bob Fosse's work in *Sweet*

Charity. All these are different styles of dance and maybe nothing like what you do, but you will remember them. They are too well structured and executed on every level not to resonate. They linger with their economy of movement, phrasing, sheer beauty, structure, musicality. All those specific masterful decisions will influence *your* ideas subconsciously because they have succeeded. They have used the art of movement to open your subconscious. And as I have stated: That is a choreographer's job.

HANDLING IDEAS

Sometimes an idea for a piece comes quickly and is executed so. Other times not, especially if you are creating a full-length production for which you will need many ideas. I start handling ideas simply by collecting and documenting them. A great addition to my way of capturing movement and sound in recent years is having an iPod or some other portable device that records video. I still write movement ideas down, but when coming back to them the magic of a phrase won't always remain when transposed into words and it requires work to re-find them. Now I film myself when a phrase comes to me. I have loads of video clips of me moving on a lawn, in the kitchen, living room. I get my kids to film me while I make their supper. I also record music ideas, a simple phrases that unless played in a particular way will be nothing special. I capture the moment. Some of the best songs ever written are sometimes only three chords. You play those chords cold there is no magic. It is the *way* they are played that makes them special, and ideas are like this. It is like recalling a dream that was amazing, but in the light of day seems empty.

Treat your ideas with respect but you need to be prepared to be harsh with them – other people are going to be when they finally appear in a piece of work. Best to audition them privately before rushing off into the studio. In general don't bolt at the start and think that everything will just fall into place because your idea is so great. Occasionally we have times when everything works and a piece is made as if with divine intervention. But here's the other scenario: you stumble into the studio, but suddenly your idea has left you. Well, it's still there but it looks a bit dull now, not so present or just a little different, a little odd... The studio is bigger than that little room where the idea came to you and a load of dancers are waiting for you to produce something. You try and remember a movement idea that was great, but it doesn't seem quite the same. Then you realise your idea only lasts about three minutes and where it goes from there you don't know, or worse, it seems to be heading for a brick wall because it had you fooled… hmm – maybe just cherish your idea a little longer before sharing it, spend some time investigating, getting to know it. Do you trust it? If that idea really has any substance that great moment will come after you've done some groundwork first.

Sometimes ideas from your subconscious come sporadically, sometimes they come as a torrent. And once they arrive, they aren't static; they have been born, they are wild and they are going to grow. They will disappear, reappear, seduce you, make you chase them, search them out. They will morph into other things, they will twist and confound you, they will merge with other ideas, they will converse with you, challenge you, and they will contradict themselves. They will swim amongst and connect those four elements: Movement, Drama, Sound and Vision. By the time you've processed ideas into a piece of work it can be impossible to remember which ideas came first as others will have pushed to the front of the queue, pretenders to the crown. An idea you had that was a catalyst, a spark of inspiration, may get discarded or lost; fail to make it to the 'final cut'. But maybe that was its purpose – to introduce other ideas. Your ideas are special but you are not the only one in the world. Everyone is special in the world to themselves. That's reality. So you must have an open mind to changing, adapting and throwing ideas away.

So document them — write them down, draw a picture, whatever you want. But then ignore them, bury them, shut them in a room for a while. Go on with your life and see what happens. If they won't leave you alone and continue to grow, then maybe they are worth looking into. Trust that ideas need time to grow by themselves without you dwelling on them all the time. There will plenty of time to do that later and you will need to work with them through all kinds of stages when you are bored and sick of them.

DEVELOPING IDEAS

This next section sounds like I am really organised, but I am simplifying the process because all the stages I'm writing about happen at the same time, jumping back and forth. I also don't do the same thing with every piece. Objectives remain but methods change.

Especially when creating a full-length production, I get some A3 sheets of paper and put down lists of ideas that have not been shelved or discarded. I stick these pages on a wall so I can stand back and look at them all. Each A3 sheet will have a collection of ideas under an umbrella of a big idea – a theme that is perhaps emerging, a feel, or in response to a piece of music, whatever... Some ideas will appear on several A3 sheets because I'm not nailing anything down yet. I may well find out I am working on several different pieces at the same time. This process reminds me of when detectives break into the hovels of deranged criminals and the walls are covered in newspaper clippings and photographs and sections torn out of the Bible or *Paradise Lost* or some other old text. These bits in cop shows and movies are often the most interesting – a reoccurring method of revealing the inside of the mad criminal's mind. So if you do a similar thing you can get a glimpse of the workings of your creative mind. (This doesn't mean you are a criminal.) And then you can start asking questions – for instance in my case – why have I several images here with mermaids? Where does this girl with a milk pail skipping over a prairie come from? Why do I keep seeing a black field with red poppies in it? This movement keeps appearing...

I really enjoy this time. Inspiration is great, maybe the most exciting part of the creative process, that moment when needles run up your spine. Enjoy this but bring each idea out into the cold light of day. Ask if you are repeating yourself. Ask if your idea is derivative. It's OK to be influenced by others' work, but your take has to be yours. I want to love an idea, but I also need to know to a point what its hinting at. I won't get all the answers; this is a good thing (what would be the point of exploring something you already know?) and intuition is as useful as objectivity. I often only realise what a section of a work is really about years after it's been and gone.

This is an insane time for me because once you give ideas a little license to occupy your mind more readily they splinter out loads of possibilities. Going back to the paper on the walls. I'd like to say this process is like watching a spiderweb being made. But it isn't. It's chaotic – more like several cracks in a windscreen, the splinters random, rapid and all over the place, connecting with each other, then splintering again. So already I'm glad I chucked some things out before I got to this stage.

I created *Made in Heaven* in 2012. But ideas for this piece developed over a number of years before this and at the same time I also wrote a novel using the same subject matter. The novel took three years. The novel and the production retained strong connections in theme, but I allowed them to set off on different paths. I guess I used ideas more suited to literature for the book and the theatrical ideas became the stage production. But I also wrote a screenplay treatment of the novel using both visuals and language to tell the story, and allowing myself to learn from the current great writing of this genre. I shelved all this writing. Maybe I'll pick it up again and try and do something with it, but all this exploration/development fed and informed the creative process and the ideas for the production. Then take into account that when I began working on the characters with a real cast, their take on the material changed everything again. This also made me go back and rewrite the novel and the miniseries… Basically the possibilities are endless.

I'm going to talk of *Made in Heaven* a little more so I can make this stage in the process as clear as possible. Here is a list of a few of the ideas for this production:

A prairie girl skipping over fields takes milk or water to a big prison warden/chief of police in mirrored shades.

Prairie girl causing trouble.

Prairie girl dreaming in the fields.

An island (hot) where you are not permitted to dream, a prison penitentiary – American.

Chain gang with bloody hoods over their heads – perhaps on a ship – a journey.

A mermaid in an electric blue sea. A girl with a red umbrella –

overjoyed, amazed but then a crazy guy wearing a hat leaps on the mermaid and cuts off its tail.

A giant great white shark attacks a boat. An electric blue sea.

A hideous he/she nun – with a rusty glove with two blades on it – it's called 'a blinder'.

Cops with mirrored shades – blind.

A broken face – a lunatic.

A sailor and a woman dance – on a ship? 1920s?

A man chases a sea-nymph type creature – they have a relationship that lasts for some time – but in the end they have to part.

A crazy hockey game played by a wild young gang – dirty – the ball is a human head – a nun's head.

A girl swings chains, a broken doll dances, pushes on though broken.

A Virgin Mary walks through the sea – vibrant blues and deep red.

A girl dances waist-high in the sea – joy, freedom....

These are only a few ideas that I had for *Made in Heaven*. There were many, many others, and many more that ended up in the novel. Here are some ideas that were discarded:

A fish tank with models of the characters and a shark in it.

A terrified wife waiting for a strange husband to return home.

The husband with a baseball bat hitting life-sized Barbie doll heads.

A detective – a script. A whole murder-at-sea story.

A scary lady on a subway train.

A childhood dream I had of a terrifying traffic warden chasing me through a forest.

I developed these ideas quite a way before shelving or burning them in my mind.

But back to the paper on the walls. Very simply I draw lines between recurring themes. Here is the list again on the next page. I'm hugely simplifying this process. Many of the ideas have other overlapping connections.

Prairie Girl skipping over fields — takes milk or water to a

Prairie Girl causing trouble   Prairie Girl Drea

An Island (hot) where you are not permitted to dream, a

A mermaid in an electric blue sea. A girl with a red
but then a crazy g
the mermaid and

A giant great white shark — attacks a boat — electric blue s

Cops with mirrored shades — blind   A broken fa

A man chaises a sea-nymph type creature, they have a rela
that lasts for son
but at the end th
to part.

A crazy hockey game — played by wild young gang — dirty — the

A girl swings chains, a broken doll dances, pushes an tha

A virgin Mary walks through the sea — vibra

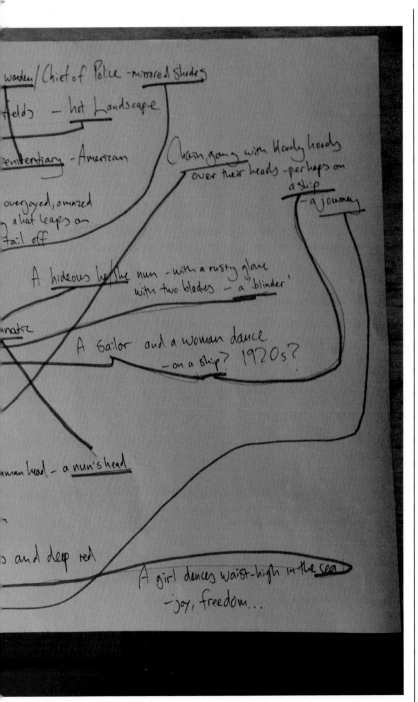

warden / Chief of Police - mirrored shades

fields - hot Landscape

penitentiary - American

overjoyed, amazed
a hat leaps on
tail off

Chain gang with bloody heads over their heads - perhaps on
a ship
- a journey

A hideous he/she nun - with a rusty glove with two blades - a 'blinder'

inmate

A Sailor and a woman dance
- on a ship? 1920s?

man head - a nun's head

and deep red

A girl dances waist-high in the sea
- joy, freedom...

I don't need to understand everything. Sorting through and developing all this material requires two sides of myself: The creature, and the pragmatist with tools to capture the magic and construct a piece of work.

Metamorphosis is always present in my work. History has told us it is present in us. We are always changing and symbolic change is a great way to show what is happening inside us. This is why I love myths, science fiction, anything that deals with this. So, I'm looking at these lists and thinking of characters, their stories and their evolution, and pretty soon my A3 sheets of paper are going to be covered with more connecting lines: Who is this prairie girl? She's dreaming, she's skipping, seemingly innocent but wild. I feel she is going to be a catalyst for change; a change in an environment where she is the trouble brewing right under the nose of the oppressor – this big cop/half android, the chief, but his name is Old He/She – because he transforms into the nun; they are two extreme sides in denial of one another, subsequently twisted and cruel. The prairie girl… she is the doll, she is the Virgin Mary, the girl set free and dancing in the sea. But she is not the mermaid. I just know this (intuition) but yes, the girl with the red umbrella who sees the mermaid, witnesses it having its tail cut off – that *is* the prairie girl – in one of her dreams. She's had a dream and… she is not allowed to. The big cop is freaking out, a status quo has been broken, and the guy who cuts the tail off the mermaid, he is one of the chain gang, a criminal, or perceived as such. And the mermaid, she is the sea-nymph, but also the woman who dances on the ship with the sailor. And these characters are the prisoners, they have escaped. They were let go by the prairie girl through her dreams. The island is a place of repression of freedom of the mind. It is Heaven, a perceived human Heaven based on manipulation and repression and fear and hypocrisy. It is dry and dead. But the sea leads to freedom, nature, wild and ruthless – great white shark. The girl's dreams are Heaven, the *real* Heaven, because it resides inside us. The island has a centre – a savage land where the nun is in charge – a hideous manmade incarnation of God, or is it the Devil, or are they the same thing? The He/She nun is trapped – both physically and inside itself. Yes it's the nun that has the boat and wants to escape. How will the nun do this? He/She needs the prairie girl. The prairie girl has a baby – with the sailor – one of the escaped prisoners.

The nun takes the baby, will claim it as its own – the son of God and a means of escape from the island it created. But you can't escape to salvation on a lie. Really the son came from a wild girl and boy, their meeting pure and savage. I need another woman in the piece – a 'savage girl'. She, the mermaid, (who I now realise represents innocence and fantasy and Eve) and the evolving prairie girl will dance as dolls to the nun's tune until they break free. And the Virgin Mary walks across the sea. Yet the prairie girl walks *under* the sea – a miracle, after the nun has been smashed off the boat and had her/his head bitten off by the shark (nature's revenge). And the cop will kick the nun's head across the stage – either as an act of ultimate denial or ignorance; and the status quo will be reestablished – but no – the prairie girl has grown up and walked away. She will shed the traditional robes of the Virgin Mary and become simply a young woman dancing in the sea. She has escaped…

I don't expect this to be easy to follow. And again I have condensed and simplified the process as, of course, it doesn't all fall into place at once, and by now characters are telling me all sorts of rubbish. For instance, the mermaid said that she waterskied off the back of the boat, which wasn't true. But you get my drift – all this is an example of how ideas run amok once you let them free.

'Stages' of development really don't have a chronological order. It's all happening at once. So here is what I am also doing simultaneously with my lists: (And this refers back to how to feed your mind and therefore your ideas and helps answer the – where do you get your ideas from? question.)

Prairie girl skipping over fields takes milk or water to a big prison warden/chief of police in mirrored shades.

'Christina's World' (1948), a painting by Andrew Wyeth. The girl at the end of *Little House on the Prairie* running down a hill, but the feel is different. I never watched any of this programme, just saw the end credits as I was probably waiting for something else to come on. Dorothy from *The Wizard of Oz*, but weirder – I see her head tilted, maybe she is a little backward or her brain has been shut down. But also I already know the dancer I have in mind for this part, that she has inspired it in the first place (not that she is backward). I know how she will do that skipping and how her stare at the audience will make them

19

wonder what she is thinking, what she is up to. I know she will know how to manipulate the audience, tell them to look where she is looking, this will be a storytelling device. She is not a victim.

Dreaming

An obvious way in for so many stories and to be used with care. The prairie girl lies in the long hot grass and dreams through the night until sunrise. She sleeps on the land. I'm influenced by Lead Belly's 'Where Did You Sleep Last Night?' – listen to it, an incredible song. I know my lighting designer will create the changing of the light beautifully. It can happen over time as the audience enter. The prairie girl is capable of murder, innocent like a cat. When she is dreaming she is being visited by 'God'. Zeus. She is Semele and Zeus is manipulating her. She is a girl in bloom. This draws parallels with the immaculate conception versus the savage, earthborn baby she has later – all those entities claiming the child. Also the scene is inspired by the Sonic Youth track: 'The Diamond Sea'.

An island where you are not permitted to dream, a prison penitentiary – American

Visions of 'Inferno'. By no means following to the letter – but levels, not in this case spiralling downwards. Three parts: The sea, the prison/purgatory, a savage land in the middle. Film: *Cool Hand Luke*.

Chain gang with bloody hoods over their heads – perhaps on a ship – a journey.

Inspired when hearing: 'Take This Hammer' by Lead Belly. Sacks over heads so they don't know where they are going. Clear Klu Klux Klan reference. Is that OK? Terrible image of slave ships. But they are also not allowed to dream (the prairie girl will remove the sacks. She lets the dreams free, causing the jailbreak).

A mermaid in an electric blue sea. A girl with a red umbrella – overjoyed amazed but then a crazy guy wearing a hat leaps on the mermaid and cuts off its tail.

The tragic Little Mermaid will be in here somewhere – but this image flashed whole into my mind – was one of the first ideas that led to *Made in Heaven* and appeared when I was creating *Love and War* (2010). I thought about it going in this production but it wasn't right so I shelved it, and it never went away or altered. I set it on stage exactly as it was in my mind. The mermaid is the prairie girl's loss of innocence, the beginning of her becoming a woman and realising her actions have consequences. The mermaid is also a 'performer' as if this is just a strange sideshow. There is irony and humour in this scene – always a good thing to have in your bag of tricks when your work tends to drift towards the darkness.

A great white shark attacks a boat. An electric blue sea.

Jaws 2. If you ever see it now you think – how did they get away with this? But this was the 1970s. *Jaws 2* is basically a slasher film for kids and the slasher is a big, hideous rubber shark. Seeing this film now I think of these teenagers – they are really young, and getting eaten in terrible, long drawn out ways. This film messed up an entire generation. But great – I get to put it in a theatre piece. The electric blue sea has something to do with rubbish VHS videos we used to hire of films in the early eighties. The colours are unreal, messed up, dreamlike. Again there is humour and entertainment in this scene.

A hideous he/she nun with a rusty glove with two blades on it – 'a blinder'

The Texas Chainsaw Massacre, Freddy Krueger – *A Nightmare on Elm Street.* In my story anyone wearing mirrored shades has been blinded by the nun. The army of cops have blind faith.

Cops with mirrored shades – blind

Films: *Westworld, Cool Hand Luke, THX 1138,* A *2000AD* comic called: *Flesh.*

A broken face – a lunatic

Inspired by the Pixies song 'Broken Face'.

A sailor and a woman dance on a ship.

Debussy's 'Clair Del Lune'. Heard it, saw it in my head. Inspired also by a duet from *Singin' in the Rain,* and by the old ballroom at the Pavilion in Bournemouth, and a Resident Evil video game set on a ship. This is a *Paradise Lost* thing also, a kind of Garden of Eden, or just about innocence and true love. It also felt like a ghost story – standing in an old ballroom imagining characters from the past.

A man chases a sea-nymph type creature, they have a relation-ship that lasts for some time but in the end they have to part.

Calypso and Odysseus. Movement material inspired by Tcherepnin's 'Cello Suite – 1. Quasi Candenza'.

A crazy hockey game played by a wild young gang – dirty – the ball is a human head – a nun's head.

St Trinian's. Mayan ballgames in which they were supposed to use human heads. But this is really about youth having no respect for tradition or age. But why should they when they are lied to and repressed by the nun/old he/she and filled with its hangups? Something about pagan revenge?

A girl swings chains, broken dolls (now three of them) dance.

Heard 'A#1' from *Volumes 5&6*, The Desert Sessions, and saw it. Then 'Pots and Pans' by The Kills and the image was there immediately. The prairie girl has been ordered to beat the savage, but it's not going to work. She has no self-regard. Tralala from *Last Exit to Brooklyn*. But in my version the dolls will triumph.

A Virgin Mary walks through the sea. Vibrant blues and deep red.

I just saw this image in my mind. Images from so many paintings. I think it connects with creating a backstory to a character we see everywhere, and finding that backstory within ourselves.

A girl dances waist-high in the sea – joy, freedom…

Down at the beach, the woman who inspired this part danced to Harry Belafonte and I thought – there is the end of this piece.

As I have said – every piece I create alters in subject and method. It became clear during the creation of *Made in Heaven* that on one level it was an ode to films that strongly affected me in my youth and through exploring this I was making a crazy kind of sense of it all. *Made in Heaven* does this more than most of my other productions. Some of my pieces have no filmic references. They are different animals. Although your work will have an identity – a voice, you want each work to lead and push you in different directions.

The process I have written about above might help you find more depth and development in your ideas, and perhaps help you get underneath them. What are they really saying? It's not always enough to just *like* an idea. When you put them all together you are making a complete piece of work. I deal with the surreal. But there is a difference between a masterpiece by David Lynch and a student film with bits and pieces of unrelated, undeveloped scraps in it. An audience will stay with you awhile when work is strange but you can't leave them behind, betray that trust, if you want them to get to the end with you. Having a great white shark come on stage is an idea I had to earn, even though I knew it would be an audience-pleaser. It had to have a reason for being there.

Now is a good time to explore reference material. If you think some old paintings are cropping up repeatedly, go and check some old paintings out. Great if you can make it to a gallery, and if not there's always the internet. There will also be a time to stop looking at these references and pursue your vision. You can easily get addicted and sidetracked by chains of research as one thing leads to another. Every time I finish a production it is very likely it will be a starting point for where I am going next. I often stumble across something very interesting and quickly shut it away because it is too massive and powerful. Another day I will look at it, but if I dwell on it now it will change too many things and I'll in fact be making another piece. Just as you can have too little content in a production, you can also get carried away with trying to cram too much into it.

Right at the beginning of the development stage, (in fact before, as I am always working on vocabulary) I will also have made another list on sheets of A3 of all the different movement I am currently working on in relation to all my ideas. I will not be structuring sections yet, but only thinking of movement styles and how to develop the vocabulary (choreographic language). The movement will be inspired by all the ideas I am working with, and also just how I am 'feeling' like moving. Even though the vocabulary will be linked with the narrative, music, emotions, visuals etc., a good piece of dance will be underpinned by a technical choreographic journey and this will require separate attention. It is very important to be thinking about this early on as it takes the longest to sort out (which is why you often see a longer work run out of choreographic steam halfway through). It takes a lot of work to make enough varied dance material to sustain a whole evening.

This is a time of absorbing and trusting intuition. I don't consider every movement and think – so what does this mean? Dance isn't like that. It is like music – you *feel* something. I never contrive a movement idea; it just comes to me. Sometimes it doesn't, I feel nothing and think – what is it I do for a living? Because today there is nothing in me at all. Then other times it pours out.

I listen to a lot of different music that is pushing itself into what I am working on. (Though, like ideas, music can be discarded over time. But if it has made you move in a certain way, develop differing material, then it will have more than served a purpose.) I will create and record material – film or write it down, but often when I enter the studio I won't refer back to it. I'm just feeling my way towards something. I won't complete anything yet. I want starting points.

If I have the luxury of some R&D (research and development) with dancers I will do some studio time. One thing that has been really helpful for me in recent years is to work with a few dancers before I have settled on any definitive ideas for a piece. This gives the chance to be inspired by movement that flowers without too many preconceptions of an outcome. This is something that I advocate for anyone.

Turning developed ideas into a piece of work

STRUCTURE

What is the purpose of structure? What defines a good structure?

For some dance-makers structure can be the primary idea, inspiration behind the creation of a work. We hear this after seeing a piece: 'I think it was about structure…' Structure may be how a particular choreographer connects with and processes movement ideas. Maybe they have isolated structure to an abstract concept in its own right, the aim not to serve an idea but an experiment to see what results when implemented to movement. I don't know, I don't work like this. Different uses of and attitudes towards structure might not resonate with me but perhaps the results will, and this demonstrates how wide an approach one can take towards the art form of choreography.

For me, structure is a tool that's purpose is to open the subconscious of the viewer and deliver what I am trying to get across. I want this to happen subtly, by stealth, not by spoon feeding information in a format that people know and feel comfortable/safe with. However, my structure *will* include tried and tested methods that have been established over time.

An audience can be aware of a structure, but I don't want them to be able to nail it down. I don't want them to be dwelling of it; they shouldn't have time to do this. If you find yourself reeling at the end of a work, that something has clicked and opened in your mind, even though you don't have the traditional things to hold onto to make rational sense of what you have experienced, then it is likely that a good structure has manipulated you. When I watched *Mulholland Drive* I was swept away, and only afterwards did I consider how its structure had driven my mind all over the place, opened my dreams and somehow made sense – not a sense I could articulate straight away, but something deeper.

As a dancer every choreographer I have worked with has structured work differently. Your way of working can be completely different to others. This is nothing to worry about. Your structure will serve your individual work, so your structure will be individual. I don't use 'maths' to structure. I've worked with choreographers that often base what they do on music structures. I do this sometimes, but sometimes not. Sometimes I write down a structure for a section of dance, sometimes I make it up as I'm going along, sometimes I do a combination of both. I use drama, theatre, storytelling, and I learnt much about these things from places outside of dance. I saw a Cunningham work the other day. I have no idea how he structured it (but if I'd danced it I would – another example of the benefits of dancing as much as you can). But the point is the structure worked. It captured me.

I write several drafts of an overall structure for a piece way before I get into the studio. The structure will contain scenes/sections, all of which will contain structures of their own. This does not mean my piece is set in stone – far from it. It is simply a blueprint from which I can move forward. If I don't have this I will leave myself a lot of work to deal with in a short period of time once the creative rehearsal period begins. I want to be armed with as much information about and understanding of my subject matter before I get on to the next stage of transferring the work from my mind into reality, because when I do that everything will shift and change again as many other factors come into play. My final structure may in fact bear little resemblance to the one I entered the studio with.

As a choreographer I have to create dance steps and an entire dance structure with music that underpins everything. This physical process will only *really* kick-off once I get into the studio with the dancers. As a choreographer I am the writer, the director, the DOP, the editor, sometimes the composer, and many other things. All these jobs require separate time and attention. Because I run my own company I have other things to contend with (it is only in the last few years that I got a full-time stage manager, so until then I was involved in that as well), all of which reach a hiatus when we are approaching the opening of a production. I will have a window of creative time to create a ninety-minute production (in this country about eight or nine weeks, though I've managed to increase this of late with periods of R&D) and my main aim during this time is to be functioning to the best of my creative ability. I need to go to that 'other place' inside myself. I don't want to be doing everything at the same time, but the reality is I *will* have to do everything at the same time. It is inevitable. But by forming a well thought through structure I can get ahead of the game.

A movie generally works something like this:

> A writer has written a script, either on demand or it is their vision. They have toiled over this script, written several drafts and finally it gets taken to the producer, director (who may already be involved), and others; basically the work gets assessed by many people then sent back for more drafts and often several writers are involved. Eventually the script is approved (months have gone by, years sometimes). The director works on this script, finding a vision for it, planning how they are going to direct it, cast it and so on – the whole shebang that a director does. The director will work on it with others: a DOP will be heavily involved, a storyboard will be drawn, costume, location, set design, light, sound, music – all creative elements are now in play and every scene will have a hundred logistical details that will need to be planned. Finally a production schedule is planned, a shoot in a number of weeks. The film is cast, rehearsed and then shot with hundreds of people making sure the director has as much peace of mind as possible and everyone they need to do other parts of the job from shooting it to making coffee. As shooting takes place more decisions will be made – lines will be cut or added, the writer on hand to make these decisions quickly alongside the director. At last the film is in the can. And the whole thing will be sent away to be edited – a whole other creative process done by experts in their field…

It is also worth noting that there is rarely, well never, a time when you are working with the budgets a film will have. In the movies entire scenes are built and shot and then thrown away without a second glance if they aren't right. If you have a big idea for a scene that requires some money you will have to be as sure about it as possible because it will be invested in; you can't say 'I have this great idea, it needs six dancers and a giant … whatever', and then realise you only need three dancers, and the giant whatever you had built isn't necessary after all. It would be great if it was possible to try out everything you have in mind without any thought of cost or logistics, but this is not reality.

I don't want to be halfway through a rehearsal process and hit a problem that is going to take a long time to sort out, if writing a structure in advance could have enabled me to foresee this stumbling block, and have a solution already up my sleeve. I want to be responsive to what emerges in the studio that the limitations of my imagination and craft *can't* foresee. These 'problems' are the most interesting; they are 'live' and in solving them I am going to learn.

Having a structure in place will enable me to start choreographing in the studio without worrying about putting it all together for a while, allowing me to immerse myself in movement creativity. The creative rehearsal process will go through many more drafts of every aspect of the work, right down to re-assessing what it is about. I will still be creating whilst working on my final edit. During this time my original structure can be referred back to when I am full of doubt or feeling I have lost the thread. It will remind me where the work came from; even if it has evolved into something else.

When forming my structure I will consider these different elements:

Narrative (not necessarily linear, sometimes only subliminal)

Choreographic vocabulary and structure

Characters

Music and sound

Visuals (including colour, costume, set – the 'world')

Symbolism

I will be considering what I am trying to say, what the whole piece is about, and how each element is subliminally nailing this into the audience; even if I don't truly know all the answers (which is almost always).

In writing all this it sounds like I have a tick-list that I just go through. I'm finding this a lot while writing this book, but, again, it isn't really like this. I *feel* my way through all these processes, my imagination has free rein and does not work in chronological order. A structural decision can catapult me back to early ideas and make me rethink them. When things are going well the structure and scenes will come from the same place as ideas. There is still inspiration, magic involved, but I have a craft watching and considering what is happening; an 'outside eye'. I don't have one method or order of structuring pieces. I spend so much time just swimming around in my thoughts and making things up, trying them out, and I create structures like this, so to suggest I work by numbers is to do a disservice to the process. It is like trying to answer the 'where do you get your ideas from?' question, as if there is one key, one secret method.

Structure doesn't have to be complicated. Sometimes very complex structures are hiding lack of content. We're not dealing with rocket science here. I always try to pare my structure down, find what I don't need, especially ideas still lingering that haven't convinced me they need to be there. Generally I can *feel* if something isn't right, though it can take time to focus on exactly what it is.

I am going to take the audience on a journey. The first three elements I mentioned above: Narrative, Choreographic Vocabulary and Structure, and Character will develop over the course of the journey, over time. The audience must be drawn into this journey. All of the elements listed above will bind together and influence each other, sometimes dictating, other times being led, and playing with this is really interesting.

Inevitably this process will end up with a timeline, a series of scenes, vital ingredients. I sometimes write my structure out as blocks of scenes on a roll of paper, like a storyboard, then pin it to the wall in the studio. Dancers can then go and refer to it, and add to it. They can also pretend to go and refer to it when they just want a little respite from me. Here is a tiny section of the timeline from *Dracula (2013)* that stretched across a wall in rehearsals. This was before the dancers began to deface it…

Narrative

Of course you don't have to have a narrative – sometimes I don't – so this starting point you can read and disregard. I have a problem with narrative: I find it hard to escape it. I can begin a piece with ideas,

ACT I

Scene 1

Dracula solo Music: String Quartet 2.1V: Lights

Allegory 1: String Quartet + Electric guitar: Fred Frith

WOLVES

Solo | wolf

2.17

Scene 2

Vampire girls rise. Dracula feeds them

F music

COITUS

Vampires coffin

3.55

Scene 3

All cast except Dracula (9)

Victorian Garden

The Brown Haired maiden

Baroque, Mina

3.33

PROPS/SET/PUPPETRY

Bag

---

3 STONE SARCOPHAGUS - on felt? pushed away at end - possibly to become part of wall + steps of set?

Bits of Dolls

Dracula leaves through arch

---

blind folds

canes

---

costume/make-up

Contact lenses, long nails, teeth, bloody dirty hands

CONTACT LENSE

WIGS

DIRTY LONG NAILS, RAGGED ROBES THEY CAN PEEL OFF

Victorian - top hats. Sh
WOMEN IN WHITE

ACT II

Scene 1

Lucy in bed

Dracula

Quincey, Helsing, Golding

maids?

Out of nar leads on Lucoweed.
Lucy maternal with vampire
6.31

Scene 2

funeral of Lucy, death of Lucy
all cast except Mina and Jonathan
rain
6 Adagio quasi unpoco 2.16
Lacrimosa Mozart 3.19

Scene 3

Mina Jonathan wedding

Allegory III. Fred Frith

Mina + Jonathan floo

4.12

Bed, Sheet

blood transfusion kit

garlic, crucifix, teeth

blood?

---

black umbrellas, veils etc
Stone sarcophagus's
stopping apl
stake hammer
blood effect, knife and rag for head.

Sheet

top hat, cane

Bouquet

---

night gown/dress

Children costume × 3 (?)

---

wedding dress

scenes that are strong and mean something. Great, I've made that piece. But now the characters are plaguing me. They tell me *that's not it, that's too easy, not enough, why don't you explore me further – I have so much to tell…* So, like a fool, I follow. And there it is again – a narrative. And at the end of the day, I love stories.

We relate to stories because they are about us. Stories that stand the test of time, are repeated in different forms, have struck a chord in our imagination, our hearts and minds. I am interested in the ancient that lives on in what surrounds us, but even more, in the legacies that reside within us. Certain stories reside in our genes, our ancestry. We return to them like children, obsessed with myths that ignite that flame of recognition of the other, the magic within ourselves. Stories are the fundamental way we learn. Children's books are a clear example of this: Why do children want you to read the same story over and over again, stories very clearly about certain things.

When I was writing my version of *Dracula* I was working with one of these classic stories to which people always return. My task was to use craft and imagination to capture that magic and communicate it to an audience. The narrative I formed was linear and strict, though I deviated from the novel – reducing the number of characters and putting in an ending of my own. In dance you have to pare plot down to essentials so you can indulge in getting underneath it all. I did the same with Homer's *Odyssey* (2016) which was a huge task. If plots are too complicated you can get bogged down with just trying to explain what is going on, and dance is not the best medium for this.

With my own narratives my task is – how far can I transcend them so they don't restrict me in utilising the forms of movement and music to their potential, and what they do best. Every work I make I deal with this task. I am drawn to Greek mythology because it transcends its narrative. I am drawn to writers that allow themselves to digress, weave away from their 'story' to explore things further. In literature this is accepted, the visual arts instantly transcend, as does music, but sometimes an audience can find this hard to deal with in dance theatre. If you deviate people say 'well what was that about?' We should be able to think of stories as a tool, a way in to what lies beyond them, what they evoke on a deeper level. I'm a bit of a martyr to this cause. In the

Western world we live in a very prosaic era, even religion is about rules. This is connected with what I wrote about not having time to think things through any more. We only think so far, not beyond. Children still have time. They are free to be distracted, go off into the other world and their perceptions can be wonderfully surreal.

At the time of writing this book I'm exploring the potential of narrative and one of my first structuring processes involves using craft to make a storyline as clear, over clear, as possible. Every scene must have a storytelling reason for its place in the work. It is a children's book. When I have created these scenes I can assess whether I have missed anything (which of course I will have). And I insist that every scene is inspired, special in its storytelling method. I put it all into a timeline and then I can mess with it, digress, but I have my skeleton structure.

At first imagine your audience is stupid. What hooks do you need to get in them to gain their interest and make them feel they have a way in, a way to understand? Ultimately you are going to leave some people behind; you can never please or interest everyone, but this is a good exercise. Never worry about whether an audience will 'like' it or not, just be clear about what you are telling them. Give them a book with pictures in it. This will also make it clearer to you. You will find something that you will suddenly realise you don't know what it is about. As I have said – you don't have to have the answers. In a lot of great work you can see the artist almost fighting with themselves, trying to push into the unknown and *this* is interesting, far more than something that is safe and just doing what it knows. Going through this process will clear some of the mud from your eyes. *Then* you can decide to make it obscure again.

Just to contradict myself and reiterate the chaotic process of creativity: You may not want to start with a narrative structure, but go straight for the subliminal – the emotional the… whatever. When writing your structure it might be completely inappropriate to have a 'story'. Not all of my work has a narrative. But whatever happens, if I put people together on stage and they move together there will be some kind of story and I will want to know more about this because it will breed movement ideas. They are living, feeling characters. Sometimes my narratives can be off the wall – a story of the mind, emotion, a dream. Dance lives in this territory brilliantly. Like a piece of music that is about a narrative, doesn't mean it has to 'tell' the story. It tells the emotional journey. So maybe fill your timeline with blocks of emotion. If you do this and then compare it with a narrative timeline you may find they are the same. The story is just weaving it together, leading from one scene to the other and taking the characters through; the characters holding the audiences' hand. These lines are blurred and my work lives in a realm that continually fluctuates between the two.

<u>Choreographic Vocabulary and Structure</u>

Each scene in my timeline will have a choreographic identity – a style with a vocabulary, and these vocabularies will influence one another, weaving together to make an overall choreographic structure running alongside the narrative (if I have one). I won't at this stage develop each vocabulary that much. I will identify starting points of movement to be explored in the studio, stemming from the content of each scene. For example: *Dracula* opens with a solo for the Count. Vocabulary to be explored: the hunter, the nobleman, a folk heritage, torment, psychopath, man and creature, vicious, dangerous, a dead man bound by his condition – lashing out at it. And, once the role is cast, I will consider what kind of material I want to explore with the particular dancer. I will consider all these movement qualities in a single scene and find connections with character and plot development in other scenes, including sections that appear at first unrelated. I will draw lines between these scenes and see what I am presented with structurally. As everything begins to bleed together the wheels are set in motion and should lead to studio time with the possibility of creating a hybrid vocabulary. It is a challenge to put this task before yourself, we all have our trademarks as choreographers but if we are to push ourselves we should use triggers that make us develop material until it becomes something else. Something we wouldn't have predicted.

Taking the *Dracula* example a little further: When I made the gypsy dance it included elements of the Count's folk material but developed in a different direction. The vampire brides were also a latent presence in this gypsy dance, as if in disguise, so I used small parts of their material here also. Material of the English Victorian characters was more classical, almost baroque in nature. When the Victorian men became more enraged and murderous their material bled into the wolves' movement. When Mina and Dracula danced together at the end of the production all the material was fused together – Mina still a Victorian woman but having tasted and become part of the darkness of Dracula's world. The whole production is connected like this and drawing lines of choreographic vocabulary connections between the scenes begins to look like Spaghetti Junction. The development needs and crossovers were prewritten in the structure (again not pre-choreographed) and were there as an almost abstract technical exercise as well as for dramatic reasons.

Like narrative or character, movement material will have to develop on its journey, but as when handling ideas, you will have to be prepared to cut it if it becomes no longer relevant to what the work is about. Choreography shouldn't be filler. You wouldn't put arbitrary lines in a script to kill time or just because you like the words. How many different ingredients do you need? Don't over complicate your dish. And if you start with too many choreographic ingredients you won't have as much time to explore each one to its full potential.

Character

Of course this goes hand in hand with narrative. Characters will go on a journey. In my work this can be pretty extreme. Sometimes things will happen to them, other times they will be masters of their own destiny. Most importantly internal things will happen and dance is the medium to express this. I wait for my characters to talk to me in my head. They tell me all kinds of things, often lies. If they don't talk to me they can be on their way. I write down what they tell me and see their journey. I look at their humanity, their flaws and their demons, what they care about, how they clumsily go for what they need and the damage they cause on the way. They grow, they lose things, they gain things, they blossom, become wise or destroyed. I *feel* their internal journey, not sit above and judge it. I relate it to myself. I see how some characters grow into beautiful things and others turn into monsters. I must care about them, and so must the audience.

I've used *Made in Heaven* as an example of turning ideas into a piece of work. In one particularly chaotic passage I wrote the beginnings of me working out a plot and character development. When I am working on structure I will refine all these ideas and create clear character journeys.

Even with an adaptation of an already-written narrative I allow the people I work with to influence and even change the actions and journey of the characters they play. Consciously and subconsciously, their own traits will inform the creation of a character, both before and when working in the studio. This is one of the reasons I do what I do; I am interested in people, finding the archetypal within them and adding their individuality into it. This is our time and our take on things, we must own our time. This connects with what I have said about being influenced by other forms of expression. Bands make music about themselves and their relation to everything and they belong in their time. I have this attitude to my company; a collection of creatures that bring something strong and different with them into the mix. I changed aspects of the role of Mina Harker in *Dracula* because I found her character in the novel did not dig deep enough relative to what she goes through. After her ordeal, her near succumbing to vampirism, the novel leaves her scarred but very much the character she began the story as. In my version Mina ends up as the most dominant force on the stage, and who or what she is now is altogether darker and more ambiguous. I also allowed the characters of the vampire brides to evolve beyond what the novel provided. I did the same with the Immortals in *The Odyssey* as well as the characters of Odysseus and Penelope.

Music and Sound

There is no definitive chronological order in which music enters the creative process. Sometimes a piece of music and its structure can be the basis of a work, the original inspiration; other times it can arrive late in the day. It is often impossible to remember when music and my ideas began to meet as this is always an ongoing process. I am often asked how I go about choosing music. I listen to all kinds of music all the time; intuition and instinct draw me to certain pieces and if they inspire ideas or connect with ideas I am already playing with I allow that music to enter the ring. When creating a full-length piece I'll be considering a lot of existing music, and pieces I might compose for each of my scenes in my timeline.

Over time I will narrow down my choices and what remains will have a powerful influence over the identity of a production. I like my musical sources to have a reoccurring, underlying presence in a production and therefore a linking structure of their own that will strengthen the foundation of the work. I will write down the structures of each piece of music I am considering so I can already be thinking of composition with the choreography. The structure of some music can be incredibly complex and intimidating and way beyond my understanding. Sometimes I will study a score, but mostly I listen and write down what I *think* the structure is – what I *hear* it to be. If I am drawn to a piece of music it will a combination of elements that have hooked me. I consider the choices a composer has made – how many instruments (ingredients), what instruments, and the approach to playing them. I identify when the music reprises motifs and melodies, develops sections, subverts them. I find it interesting with music based on written scores how different musicians play them – speed, attack, variation of rhythm and the liberties they take. It can be the same as seeing different actors approach the same script.

It is not enough to simply *like* a piece of music; I have to have a strong idea worthy of it. The music has to marry with what I am trying to achieve, and work in my timeline. I will consider the pace, colour, style, length of each piece of music and how they all sit together as scenes. I consider how much I want to follow a piece of music's structure or at times work against it, go through it. Often the structure of each scene in my timeline will be rooted in the structure of the music I intend to use for it. It is uncanny how a musical structure can sometimes tell the same 'story' that I want to convey.

If I have a series of scenes in which I feel my musical choices, although saying what I want them to say, are too much on a similar dynamic level, I will try to counteract this. I need variation and I will likely have several different pieces competing for the same scene – music that expresses the same subject matter, but in different ways. I have put vastly different types of music into productions – from Sonic Youth to Mozart. This is always carefully considered and never just for effect.

When working to a strictly paced narrative I may have a great track of music that sets an energy completely suited to a scene, but the track is too long, the scene has said what it needs to, and I have the rest of the track left over. Do I develop this section of choreography? Or do lose the music and rework the scene with something else, or cut some of it (I avoid doing this if I can). Does a piece of music absolutely nail an emotion I am trying to achieve or is it too strong? Can I match it, can I add anything to it that it isn't already saying? If both the choreography and the music say the same thing will it make the scene overstated? This is a very common trap to fall into.

I will consider a through-line of sound in my timeline. Sound in film is as important as the visuals. My work is film on stage. Sound will bind everything together – right down to the scene changes. It can be used subtly – the audience hardly aware that it is there. More often than not there will be a soundscape present when the audience enter the auditorium. This sets everything up, creates the world they are about to enter, so ideas about what these sounds might be are a fundamental structural decision.

<u>Visuals – (including colour, costume, set – the 'world')</u>

The first draft of my work is a movie in my mind. At some point I have to be realistic about the fact I am not shooting a movie – it's all going to happen on stage with costumes, set and lighting, and always a lot of smoke. Writing my structure will make me create a rendition of my 'movie' with the tools at my disposal. I will already be in discussion with my creative collaborators so their prime source of information will be the 'movie', but already I will be translating this for stage. I will tell them what I see in every scene and list all the prop, set and costume ideas. My collaborators will take the basis of this world and are free to explore their ideas. I am specific but not so specific that they can't have freedom and do what they do better than me. Then we'll start to pare it all down, see how we can create this world. So this structure is both an artistic vision and a practical tool from which to proceed. And this all happens now, before I have started rehearsals. Collaborative input is essential at this point, it helps me know if my ideas make sense and where we might be heading in the design, and anything that is going to be really tricky – say, a very fast costume or set change, so I can be prepared for this, already thinking of solutions.

Symbolism

Symbolism walks hand in hand with dance; it can be at once specific and ambiguous, ask as many questions as it answers, and transcend words. A whole world, state of being, idea, juxtaposition, cross-reference can be created with one symbol. With storytelling it's my first port of call, so often better than simply acting things out (sometimes not). It is an essential element of my structure alongside all the other methods of communication to be employed. Symbolism can shock an audience, propel them beyond their preconceptions and remind them that dance is a powerful art form. Map out your symbolism, when and how you will use it, when you will return to it. If you are canny the audience will get it, will go with you without having to translate it into something cerebral; like the women pumping their fists to The Kills' 'No Wow' in *Sea of Bones* (2006). So many people who saw this said 'I want to do that move' because it *meant* something – they felt it and wanted to experience doing it. As with stories and characters that touch us deeply, so do symbols because they represent unifying things.

There are loads of established symbols out there but I like discovering my own. Symbols are like ideas, emerging suddenly from the subconscious, and open to interpretation. I often incorporate them in a work long before I know what they mean to me. Symbols emerge throughout the entire creative process. In rehearsals it is almost as if a certain amount of work, a certain amount of ritual, has had to have been done before they reveal themselves. Most of the characters in my pieces are symbols of something, as are their actions. *Love and War* (2010) had only a hint of narrative and was rooted and structured with symbolism: Tying Aphrodite up in rope while she rotates in a pair of very high heels, performing gestures of all forms of love until the rope simply falls away. A mother creating a nest of dragon's teeth around her children. A giant spider killing a God of War in a bath. A girl eating an ice cream after a movie massacre in a parking lot. A tiny music box as a glimmer of hope and beauty in the dark. A girl walking a tightrope while her parents watch. (And interestingly I instinctively made this production in the round.)

My production of *The Odyssey* is littered with symbols. It had to be to tell such an epic and universal story. Here is how I used one symbol

to show the passing of time and what twenty years of waiting for her husband did to Penelope.

TIMELINE

I will have two timelines – one crammed with information and so messy only I can understand it, and another that I will take into the studio. This won't be overloaded with detail, it will be pretty simple – choreographic material to be explored, music, and a basic run down of the narrative. A kind of 'need to know' for the cast. I don't want them going off on a tangent just yet. I'll also put down set, costumes, light, puppets, masks; any relevant practical information for each scene.

I will attempt to view a first draft of a structure for my work with an outside eye. Every section or scene will affect the one adjacent to it but also every other section/scene in the whole production. You can be struggling with say, the final third, but find the solution is something that needs to be changed in the first third. For instance – a bit of information you could give that means when it comes up again later the audience will already have some knowledge about it. An obvious example of this is when a story starts with the end. There may even be something you can tell at another time which means you can remove it completely from another section.

I think of 'islands'. Subliminal markers on a journey. The audience has reached somewhere. They have a moment, sometimes only a breath, then they are sent on their way again with the information they need to embark on the next part of their journey. This island may involve a small reprise and development of material they have seen already but need a small reminder of. Music does this with a repeated motif. The islands don't mean respite; I have a rule with myself – I should be able to drop into any point in a production and it should captivate, be strong in its own right, not just a link to another section. This is not easy to achieve and there will always be the best scenes in a work, but it's good to aim for. There are some books that you can open at any page and they will hook you straight away. *On the Road* by Jack Kerouac or *Cannery Row* by John Steinbeck do this for me. I go to these and other books when I'm feeling a little uninspired, open a random section and the flame in me is reignited immediately. Work like this is my benchmark. It makes me feel I can always do better.

There are all kinds of structures used in novels, music, film. A lot of film struggles because it gets stuck in its two-hour format. This is why we can lose interest and think – well I kind of know what is going to happen now. I think this probably has a lot to do with some unimaginative producers or studios demanding a certain product they know they can sell. But the reason this format is there is that it has been proven to work and there are still so many great films being made that manipulate this structure, still surprise and lead us into the unknown. However, every time you make a new work why not try and push yourself? What is the point of doing what you know? Well, you can earn a living, and I don't undervalue this.

I think it is an exciting time for screenwriters when it comes to miniseries. There are more possibilities for structure that doesn't follow a single format. It must be liberating, like novels that can be whatever length, structure they need to be. But again – airport novels tend to follow the same structures, and it's interesting that in popular culture many people want what they know. So it's good to accept that established structures do work and if you are shrewd you can use them to your advantage. James Bond films are a typical example in this. Start with an action sequence (often the best part of the film) which throws the audience in at the deep end. It's a simple tool. I guess we feel safer when we know where things are going. It opens a door and says 'step inside'. Certain devices can seduce the viewer into your world, and then you can shut the door behind them. You don't have to start with a big explosion, but you want your first image to capture, intrigue, lead. Try out a known structural opening but subvert it. Imagine the audience doesn't trust you, or has just had a bad journey across town or an argument with their partner and are just not in the mood. Try and blow their mind on several levels, quickly, but don't rush it – contradiction I know. They have to be hit with a visual punch, movement that is sure of itself, characters that somehow they feel empathy for very quickly. Refine the elements you think you want to use, then you can make them great with your cast.

I draw a simple pace graph of my timeline showing high and low moments. Have you got a whole chunk of scenes with similar pacing? Again – look at a James Bond film. Action, plot, character, shower scene; action, shower scene, plot, sinister action, plot, big action… something like this, anyway. And studying other successful structures doesn't have to be a chore – study something that you enjoy, are moved by. So, sitting through your favourite boxset is not a guilty pleasure. It is work. *Game of Thrones* has taught me many things.

If I'm going to inflict a heavy sequence on the audience – something dark and perhaps disturbing, if I continue to batter them with this they will become inured to what I'm saying. So it's good to think up some 'sweeties' that you can give out at various times – so long as they don't compromise the work. They won't necessarily lessen the impact of what you are trying to get across; they can enhance it. A set piece, a visual feast, humour, irony are all good. Sweeties are good, and not as easy to create as one might think. You can say something subversive and dark with them, like a woman with giant spider-legs eating someone in a bath. Humour (one of the greatest and most underrated of art forms) is a great structural device. Think of scenes of humour and irony that appear in Shakespeare's tragedies. If it was a good enough device for him, why not consider it yourself?

Identify a blockage. Imagine your structure as a tower of cards. Something is really bothering you, almost to the point of chucking the whole thing away. Try removing one of the bottom cards, a scene you believe is the basis of the whole piece. Now surely the whole stack is going to collapse. But wait – somehow it doesn't. What you thought was the foundation, the thing supporting your structure is an illusion. What you thought was essential is actually a hindrance to the work growing and becoming what it is meant to be. (Alternatively – I had a piece I worked on, hacked and hacked away at, and never completed because I couldn't identify what was wrong with it, drove the dancers up the wall I'm sure. Eventually I pulled all the lower cards away: music, narrative, everything. This time the whole thing *did* collapse and I chucked it all in the bin, except one little bit which went into another piece and fitted fine. But this was a disturbing time for me when I thought that was it – I'd lost it – would never choreograph again. Just so you know – we all feel like this sometimes.)

I often find my structure takes on a kind of mirror form, like those paintings we did at school – paint one side of the paper then fold it in half to print the other side. Often, years later, I see mirrors in pieces that I didn't even know were there. I find most scenes will have a partner on the other side of the halves where a character, choreographic motif, music, anything, returns and is developed. (This doesn't mean you have to have an interval to have two halves.)

I time keep, add up the minutes so I get an idea of length. If I feel I've said what I want in thirty minutes either there is a big development missing or I'm simply working on a thirty-minute piece. I often see twenty-minute pieces that I think have said what they want to in ten minutes. Sometimes even five minutes.

Consider the theatrical and choreographic style of each scene and the world you are creating. Do you have one unifying style or are you going to try to fuse different ones together? I mix eras and worlds because my mind sees everything juxtaposed. It is the same as using diverse musical choices; if the content and drive is right it can be possible. You can take different theatrical styles and mix them up in one scene. You can cross over – take a piece of music and change the dance vocabulary or theatrical world usually associated with it. This doesn't have to be extreme, sometimes it is just a subtle bleeding in of something else. This can create something that is not easy to define, that stands in its own right. It's been done throughout the evolution of music. I think it could be explored more in dance.

I consider 'passing the baton' – the way each scene moves on to the next. Sometimes I want a smooth transition, sometimes I want to destroy what has gone before. In *Love and War* a beautiful, sad solo to a Tom Waits song was followed by a cheerleader stomping on and chewing gum. The transition was more than simply moving from one scene to another; it symbolised that in life someone can open their heart and you can feel empathy for them, then it can seem foolish because the world is harsh and doesn't give a shit.

How long are your scenes? Movies sometimes start with lots of chopped up images (sometimes not) but plays tend to begin with a reasonably long scene. Sometimes I try to fuse lots of short scenes into one, especially at the beginning. If your material is connected maybe it can all be said in one go. The opening scene for *Dracula* is a combination of several scenes or events: the Count in the woods; the entrance of the wolves; the stolen baby, the peasant woman begging for it back, killed by the wolves; Dracula returning to his vampire brides and giving them the baby to eat. These events began life as separate ideas, but I made them into one nine-minute scene because they all had the same aim: introducing Dracula and his world. The Count connected the scenes until he 'handed the baton' to the vampire brides at the end. I covered what was needed: the Count and his many qualities, his story, his wolves, his location; the existence and state of his vampire brides; I introduced the choreographic vocabulary associated with all these characters and creatures; and I set up the dramatic fusion of different theatrical styles: old storytelling theatre with traces of an old silent movie but bleeding into something real because the events are horrific and followed by the terrible screaming of the vampire brides. The visual presentation is filmic, we have lightning and thunder (a sweetie), and two contrasting pieces of music (a theme written for acoustic guitar and Ligeti's 'Atmosphères for Orchestra'). There is also symbolism: vampires lying on coffins face-down – buried facing Hell; wolf heads that will appear subliminally throughout the production. Then consider the scene that follows, linked by a storm opening into evening sunshine and the sound of birds singing – a duet between Mina and Jonathan in a Victorian garden – another world, another choreography, another music, their young love, innocence. We have established two worlds side by side that we know are going to come together in the plot. If the choreography, narrative and characters are strong and clear alongside all the other decisions (theatrical style, music, etc.) the audience should be captured and ready to come on the journey with you. This example shows how every element and craft I have written about so far has been incorporated and fused together to create one entity.

You won't form your structure all in one go. You won't solve its problems by just sitting in front of it 24/7. You need to trust that if you take a break from it it will continue processing inside you. Give it time to grow on its own accord. You can wake up one morning and something you were struggling with will have been solved while you were asleep. Solutions can also come from the world outside your self-obsessive bubble. Very often something my kids say to me will present me with the simplest of solutions or perspectives.

I want to set everything in motion and see where it takes me before I write a conclusion for my piece. Do I even want a conclusion? Sometimes no conclusion is a conclusion. Like in life. But I cover myself. I wrote several endings for *Dracula* even though I knew I wasn't going to decide what it would be until I had created the first three quarters of the production. Where do all the journeys end up in your imagination? Write all the possibilities down – choreographic, character, plot… then shelve it. Get in the studio and see what happens.

The creative rehearsal process

I love writing because I am self-reliant. I'm not wasting anyone else's time, or money. It's just me, my trip, my vision, my learning, exploring, tackling; my own limitations; and in the end only myself to pick up the pieces if it goes wrong. It is a fantasy I have to one day wander the world and write about the strange things going on in my head, free from all responsibility that comes with trying to create these things on stage. With my company a production can involve up to fifty people. Not as many as other projects one can be involved with, but still, there are a thousand pressures and things that can go wrong in all aspects of the work, artistically and logistically, and ultimately I am responsible because I have put together the machine to fulfil my vision. One of the reasons I am prepared to go through all this stress is the people I work with. Throughout life we find others we connect with. I have, and continue to fill my company with these people. We create something together, and I learn from them. Choosing whom you work with will form the foundation of your final product. It will determine the state of your mental and physical health and therefore your ability to function as an artist. If this goes wrong the whole experience can be traumatic. Get your team right, from administration to producers, production management, set, costume, lighting design; music, sound, publicity, photography, P.R, marketing and everything else. And ultimately the casting of your performers is everything.

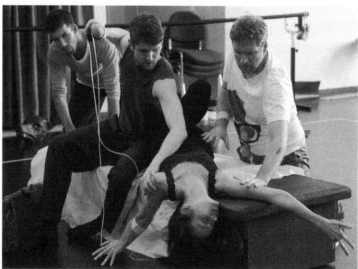

I have worked with dancers, actors, singers, musicians; professionals, students and amateurs. Mostly I work with professional dancers, and this is what I am going to write about, but there are things to be learnt from other disciplines – particularly the way actors work, and the best results come through a combination of approaches. There are plenty of things said and written about actors and in comparison dancers don't have much of a voice. You need to understand the discipline and the animal you are working with. You are going to have to communicate with them. Directors and choreographers need to be psychologists. They need to tap and grow something within artists in an environment of vulnerability, fear, stress, pressure – you name it, on both sides.

Like Achilles, dancers burn bright and brief. They are nomadic. They have old-school skills, nothing a computer can shortcut. I often say we are like a travelling sideshow moving from town to town and putting on our weird shows. In this sense not much has changed about the profession in a world where so much has changed and so much is lost. Similar to musicians, dancers' expressions transcends words. They are intuitive. They have chosen an expression that involves quite a lot of pain. At times they survive on adrenaline and physically pushing through when they are exhausted because they are trained to do so. They are often compared to athletes, but, although dancers train to be the best they can, their aim is mastering their physical and artistic potential as individuals. It is not about who is the fastest or the strongest or about winning.

Starting an ambitious project can be like staring up at a mountain you are about to climb, the top out of sight. You have to be patient. You have to be positive. We adhere to an attitude in my company: never let the first reaction to something we are going to try to achieve be – I don't think it is possible. Think – how can we make this possible? That costume, make-up change, along with a set change and crossover in under thirty seconds? Let's see what we can do…

A plane flies across the sky. How is that possible? The city you stand in – how was it built? How was Stonehenge achieved, the Pyramids, a cathedral, a bridge – any monolithic structure built before modern engineering? All things start with dreams. In our case no one need sacrifice their life to make it happen so surely there are ways to make a dream a reality. It's hard

work, but probably not as hard as a child going down a deadly coal mine, breathing in fumes and dust for twelve hours straight with no chance of a future and death lurking in the darkness; or the eternal quest for freedom of the oppressed or... well any other of a million examples of what people on this planet have to do or have done.

During the rehearsal process dancers get tired, you get tired. Tiredness will affect your perception of what you are doing, and your inspiration to make material. It is very easy to call it a day when you feel this. Sometimes it is good to leave things, come back to them fresh the next day. But sometimes it is important to push through fatigue; you may get a second wind later in the day and make something good in the final half hour of rehearsals. Don't lose your discipline. As a dancer you are tired most of the time, but you have to drive on, and this increases your stamina. Over time you get stronger, can do more, and your dancing improves. As a choreographer you will find out how you work best, how many hours a day suit you. But don't give in too easily. We only find what we are capable of when we push ourselves.

You must learn how to communicate with those you work with. You must find your own way of doing this just as you must find your own work. With choreography there is physical demonstration, then a technical breaking-down of material – tell dancers what you are doing and identify what they are doing. In giving dramatic information consider what will resonate with the individual. Will a dancer respond best to verbal or movement direction? Consider if you need to work on your verbal communication. I like to see if dancers do what I say and *feel* their way in, whether they will capture what I am looking for. That way I know if the lines in my 'script' are right before information follows. Too much information can complicate things. I want just enough to put dancers in the right zone, and work with the creature. I've seen situations in which dancers are given a whole tonne of information and then have no idea what to do, or they start trying to interpret it, putting things on top of a shaky foundation.

Every dancer I work with will be different. I communicate differently with each one. I know what pushes their buttons, what will elicit a creative response and what information won't be of value. Some dancers break down what I am doing technically very quickly; some just go for it and instantly become a character – that is their way in. Both are interesting, and the end result will involve both approaches. When I'm showing a new phrase to a group, some dancers will be at the front, getting it fast, and nailing it. Some dancers will be at the back doing... I don't know – but I do – they are working in their way. This is great, and I can't wait to see what is growing in everyone.

I'm terrible at having too many people in the studio working on different things. I end up jumping from person to person when I should be focusing on one thing. It is good to send some dancers away, sometimes, so you have a little peace to work on one thing without distraction. It is also good to schedule a day, then everyone can organise their concentration. I am also bad at doing this, mostly when I'm creating material because I have no idea what is going to happen in me from one minute to the next. But once you begin putting things together you can be more organised in this department.

When you make work you are vulnerable; you have to open up and bring something inside you out into the world. You have to be strong in your convictions, and you need armour to protect you against the knocks you are going to take. You have to be open and tough at the same time. I don't like bossing people around, I have no interest in this but I have to do it. I have to have an ego. I don't like having an ego, but it is a prerequisite of what I do. Forces both outside and within are going to test your belief in what you are doing. I often wonder why anyone on earth would be interested in what I do – but if I dwell on that I won't make anything.

I run my company how I want to run it because it is mine. I built it. I expect dancers in class every day. Class is a ritual and making work requires ritual to get the mind and body in a collective zone. Keep your dancers fit; know they have done class to maintain and improve technique, build strength, get the heart going, dance together. After a previous day's work dancers will be feeling sore, they will be uneven; they will need to straighten, align their bodies again to prepare for another day. In doing class the dancers are supporting each other and creating a unity as everyone struggles to get the machine, the tools in working order. If dancers turn up when they want and don't do class, the ritual is broken. It also sets off a mentality: *if they aren't doing class, why should I?* Or *that's not fair, I'm in so much pain this morning the last thing I want to do is class, so why are they not doing it?* Or *how come this dancer doesn't seem to think they need to do class, do they think they are better than me?* This may seem childish but subconsciously these things ripple and it isn't a good start to the day. People are injured sometimes, or just taking care of things, so there is a little deviation from this. If a dancer doesn't want to do class because they really know it is not a good idea on a particular day, I expect them to let myself and the teacher know. This is an acknowledgment of respect for the ritual. It is simple and clear.

Dancers should work on material without me telling them to do so or hold their hand through the process. A dancer shouldn't just do a phrase a couple of times and think that's it. Dancers need to get material in their bodies and explore its potential; they are the ones who will eventually go on stage and dance it. I expect dancers to get going after a break without me saying 'why don't you work on such and such a phrase'. They should already be doing this. This also allows me just to watch what is going on in the room and think about what I am doing, rather than – why is that dancer not doing anything? I've just taught them a load of movement and they are showing no inclination to work on it.

All the dancers in my company know these expectations. And they get on with it. If I invest time and care in a dancer – a person – I expect the same in return. If a dancer isn't of that mentality that's fine – just don't come and work with me. I want an artist who is serious and interested in what they do, who is on a personal journey with their relation to the art form. If all this is in place we are working together in a positive environment with the potential to produce something great. In my opinion the whole shebang is too much hard work to do anything but this. Life is short – this is our time. And this does not mean the working environment is deadly serious and hushed. There is a lot of humour in the process. And this is just as important as everything else.

Creating a role with a dancer is collaborative and there is an unspoken understanding of finding something together, pushing into the unknown. Normal relationships and friendships often don't achieve this. Life is isolating sometimes; connecting on a deeper level with people makes it less so, and I think this is part of what making work is about. Often we sense what we are doing is important, but only years later, when we look back at our careers, do we realise how special a particular time was and how it added to who we are now.

Dancers are trained to take direction and in general execute what you initially want very quickly. The saying goes: Tell a dancer to go and stand in one corner of the stage and they'll do it; tell that to an actor and they'll say 'Why?' Of course there is a generalisation here, but being trained as a dancer I have much of a dancer's mentality in the way I create, and I begin by going about getting some 'pictures' pretty fast. I start making movement and putting people on the canvas, so to speak, arranging where they are going to be in the space and what they are going to do. If I am making a piece on a rep company, on a first day I'll just start working. None of the dancers will know what it is they are working on (they might not even know who they are working with because some dancers are complete space cadets). They won't be asking – who am I in this piece? We'll begin exploring the movement and they will get a feel of what it is about. They will trust that information will come along the way. This is very similar to a musician trying to find a riff and a groove and others listening and playing with it until it becomes something.

Actors often begin with discussion, information, a read-through of the text, whereas dancers are up on their feet immediately. Dancers will do class, they will have broken through into the day and be ready to go. I don't want them all warmed up only to sit them down for a few hours of discussion. Do that and half of them will fall asleep. Keeping the engine running will be more productive. I'm generalising again (impossible not to do this when trying to get a point across) – actors have all kinds of ways in to their process, and sometimes you may need to start with words, especially if you are not actually making your own material. But establishing the physicality of your piece will be your foundation, and initially words can sometimes get in the way of this.

As work progresses in the studio many other factors and demands will come into play, and then dancers will be pushed into thinking beyond how they have been trained. I have learnt so much from working with actors and it is my hope that by the time I have finished working with a rep company that some of the dancers will have added information, knowledge and skills to the way they approach their work. There is often debate as to what skills dancers should have when they graduate from training. My dance training was simple – it was hard and relentless, it was about technique, the grounding. Technique in itself takes years of training, there is little time for anything else. Afterwards you go and work for a choreographer. You see the way they and their dancers work, and you learn. I had no idea how Anne Teresa De Keersmaeker worked but I joined Rosas and found out. She obviously saw the potential in me. I don't expect a dancer coming out of college to know exactly how I work or to have all the skills I've spent a career acquiring. I expect intelligence, an open mind and a capacity to learn. Give me a dancer with a strong basic technique, a hunger and instinct for drama, and the potential to connect their animal with their training, and that something special that no amount of training can achieve. I'll do the rest. It's part of my job.

I started my company so I could make the productions I want to make and I fill it with dancers who are drawn to and understand how I work, so together we can continue to explore and grow. It is different to working with a rep company – when a dancer in my company knows they are cast in a piece they will be on to me – is there anything they need to read, films to see, imagery; anything they can research about their character so they can start thinking about it? They want information. And often they will find connections and references of their own. But again, when they enter the studio they won't be talking immediately about this. Their trust lies in the process, that things will begin to reveal themselves when they and myself are ready. I may give bits of information as we work but at first everyone will be so busy trying to get their bodies into the choreography they will only be asking physical questions.

I'm not looking for perfect technique in a dancer, but those who have the maturity to adapt what they have to their body and use it well. I'm interested in mongrels. I was a mongrel as a dancer. I worked hard but wasn't good enough in many of the techniques I learnt to do them in their purest form. I started dancing late and have had to learn to work with my limitations, in fact use them to my advantage. No two dancers in my company are the same. Other companies may look only for a particular type of dancer because they work with a different aesthetic. Whether you do this or not is your choice dependent on the kind of work you want to make. I have some core dancers that I have worked with over the years, some come and go, some stay for long periods, and new ones come along, but every piece I make is like a film or a play and I will be sure I have a part for whomever I cast.

As well as the dancer I am interested in the *person* that enters the studio. It's all part of the same package. Glimmers of things inside them that we can create characters and journeys from; elements *they* are instinctively drawn towards. I tend to see this in dancers very quickly; the animal is apparent and I know whether there is something there that interests them and me. Looking at and sensing the creature before you is one of the first vital processes of choreography, and that means everything – it can just start with the eyes. Imagine your favourite movie actor. See a closeup shot of them. Their eyes will tell you so much. Things like this are a gift – that magic I keep going on about, coupled with technique, and a gift for you to use at your will. Think how you can use and challenge a dancer's ability and qualities.

A room full of special dancers is like handling too many ideas. You are going to see what seduces you but you must stay true to what you are trying to achieve. You may make a beautiful sequence on a dancer, but if there isn't a place for it in the work you might have to lose it. I could put together a whole evening of things I have cut from a work that are special. But making that beautiful sequence will feed your finished product even if you don't use it in its initial form. It is a sketch, and will also get the dancer moving, suggests traits of their character; the language beginning to inform their body and mind. This takes time, even when the dancer has worked with you for years. The physical process will get everyone in the zone you have been living in for months. It will also warm *you* up. Within a few days you will be getting to grips with the material you are making, developing it, and seeing it on others for the first time.

I work pretty fast, but not on purpose, and sometimes I consciously slow myself down. When you start on a big production it is tempting to rush because there is so much to be done. But trust your homework, you should already be ahead of the game so you should have earned time for things to evolve. If you push the beginnings too early it can be like lopping off a bud before it has had the chance to flower and show you what it truly is, something that you perhaps never imagined, but giving you what you want. Something that is going to change the work.

Creating movement

On a first day in the studio I'm so loaded up with information most of the time I have no idea what I'm going to start with, right up until after class. It depends how I feel. There are so many possibilities and already all the dancers around me and all the things I can do with them is messing with my head. Sometimes I just go ahead and make the piece in my mind, start at the beginning and work through. But these days I tend to begin with just movement, not in any set order, just finding a language, a vocabulary. And this is the process I'm going to write about.

The first port of call, and the most allusive thing to tap, in the studio, is simply whether you are in the state of being of the animal that is going to create good movement. Attaining this is always unpredictable and inconsistent, you have good days, OK days, and bad days, though through experience you get better at finding it within yourself – what to shut off, what stimulates you.

Here are two contradictory things I do simultaneously: I don't 'think' when I first initiate movement. I tap into the feeling of what I am going to express. I earn this indulgence through my preparation. That work is inside me. Now I can move from the heart – cross over to the primal power of movement that transcends cold conscious thought. Now the contradiction – I *do* need to think. Let's go back to my introduction to choreography – Muhammad Ali; when he was in the ring he wasn't just the fighting animal; he'd use his mind at the same time, making decisions, analysing ways to outsmart his opponent; he would utilise his craft alongside all kinds of tricks – physical, mind games – watch the film *When We Were Kings*. The trick is to have the mind and body working in tandem.

PHRASING

So I make some phrases. Often without music. And often, at first, slowly. Every detail of a phrase must be explored; every accent and articulation. A phrase must have a 'musicality' of its own, a rhythm and a melody, even if the rhythm is subliminal. It must make sense like a sentence, and any clutter should be removed from it. No element can be vague and it must have subtlety. I will identify the attributes of the overall physical identity of a phrase – something is going on, a feeling in how I'm dancing it, for instance – I'm being hooked by something and dragged and at the end of each move I'm retracting back... The hook feels sharp, bubbles streaming out behind me as I get dragged and the resistance I give makes me feel like I'm underwater. When I'm released I retract through my bones and the next move of the phrase comes from this, and I'm allowing myself a moment of no control over the next move I make, almost falling into it, and this sets up the next 'line' I hit. This is the animal talking, while my mind will work out what I am doing technically with my body. I identify where each movement is coming from – the impulse – and become more specific about the accent, find out what its potential is. Often I will find that the impulse isn't even coming from me – it is like something external is hitting me, pushing me, I am receiving something *other*. Where does movement *really* start? Never forget you are touching those invisible powers, spirits, ghosts, ancestry deep inside you, and from the world outside. The same place those ideas come from. When a movement really takes me at first I have no idea where it comes from. It hits me before I can think. But all this has to be eventually broken down technically so you can communicate this information to your dancers.

LINE

Line is an essential part of the identity of a phrase. Line or 'picture'. When you are dancing you are constantly creating pictures in the viewer's mind. Sometimes these are obvious, sometimes they are almost subliminal. Things they will remember. These pictures will tell them something – abstract or literal. Let's look at some pictures. My phrases will be peppered with these pictures/lines – what do they say?

Or very different – using much more traditional lines:

All your decisions will log inside the viewer and will form the basis of what they are experiencing. You are guiding them, manipulating them. Line means anything – from a traditional dance position to something as small as the tension in someone's fingers; where someone is looking (look at the last image above – how different would it be if both dancers were looking out towards the audience?). Small details can completely change a viewer's perception. Often when revisiting a phrase and finding that it it isn't working like it did can be because some of the 'pictures' are a little out of focus. We can see this immediately in ballet – if someone doesn't hit that arabesque the moment is lost. This works in the same way with every picture you create. A simple exercise – do a phrase with you eyes looking down, then with your focus out. It changes what the phrase communicates. Even simpler – hold out your hand with your palm open, look into your hand, look away from your hand, look towards the audience, does this suggest giving? Does it suggest it more if you look towards the audience, or does it become begging? Open your other palm, so two hands now, a subliminal image of Jesus Christ? What if you are on your knees. Now do all this with clenched fists. What does that say? Any line you are hitting – what is it? Can you make it clearer, better? Do you want to alter it, maybe extend it?

DEVELOPING MOVEMENT VOCABULARY

Having been through the process above and narrowed down the elements of a vocabulary I am exploring, I will limit myself to these ingredients and make some more phrases in the same style. Then I'll break these phrases down again, push some of the attributes and all the time work on technically isolating the impulses of the physical identity, the accents and details so I can get rid of any physical clutter around them. This is the same process you go through as a dancer – only using what one has to in order to execute a phrase. I am refining all the time; even if the phrase is like a rag doll being dragged around by its hair – you want it to be only that – no mud in it. Although that's quite a nice idea – a rag doll and some mud. I sometimes do this – add a wildcard into the phrase, see what that does to its identity.

By releasing the parts of the body I don't need to execute a movement I can either do nothing or possibly something else with them. I will also try using the same impulse from different sources in the body. I will challenge, change the direction of a phrase, stop the flow through a movement and take it somewhere else, change the attack, where the commas are, or hit one accent a little harder than before – anything that makes it less predictable. A viewer will 'see' all this work, even though they won't *see* it. I will experiment with the speed of the phrase as a whole, but also with acceleration and deceleration within the 'melody', and this will again pose all sorts of questions and choices. I'll chop the phrases up and combine them with each other. And I'll find motifs that seem to be reoccurring; possibly a move or a line that seems to epitomise the identity of the material.

I will begin transposing some of the phrases, make versions on the floor, on the knees, maybe retrograde them (do backwards). Transposition is one area in which I sometimes take more of a backseat nowadays; I've done so much floor work and backwards material over the years that I am more interested in observing what the dancers do when they take this on. Because the material being transposed is already specific, the dancers will have certain rules and parameters that they will need to apply to their transposition.

While developing a specific vocabulary, possibilities to take the movement somewhere else will come up, and it is likely that I will start working on some new phrases based on what I have unearthed. This can mean I am working on three or four differing movement vocabularies at the same time. This is already the beginnings of crossing over to other styles that I will develop for other sections of the production, or perhaps not; I am being indulgent at this stage, almost developing movement for movement's sake, simply exploring. I keep an eye on this, we are getting a motor running but I could go on indefinitely and this can get like handling too many ideas. If I set off on too much of a tangent my subject matter will become distant. My preparation is always questioning what I do, though I sometimes tell it to shut up because I feel I'm onto something as a pure 'maker of movement', a choreographer practicing, extending and developing vocabulary.

I always feel the floor when I dance, either under my feet or any other part of me that has contact with it. A phrase must find its grounding. I will make it heavy, too heavy, just to find where I am putting my weight, and build strength. We have hundreds of different muscles, bones; every movement will demand a different combination of these, and you have to train those muscles up so they can execute power and stability into the movement. A movement may gain so much power after doing this that it unleashes a jumping phrase. Any phrase made gently may become very fast or physical, and I want to know where I will be pushing from. The floor is your partner, you can't dance without it, so use it. It is a very reliable partner. It is always there.

Say you are looking for a 'hard' phrase, something physically powerful, or maybe a fast phrase, or something full of anxiety. That doesn't necessarily mean you should just catapult yourself into trying to get this based on a ferocious energy. Often a phrase that looks fast or hard in my work will have been made gently. Clear articulation will achieve a sense of speed, better than if you just race through a phrase with tension and no detail. I learnt early on in my dancing career, when asked to make very physical material and repeat it for long hours in rehearsals, that I had to find a way to do this without destroying my body. I saw how more experienced dancers around me were doing this, and I made sure that everything I made was organic. That doesn't mean floppy or without using muscle or power. But I made clear pathways, and although the material was highly physical and could even appear dangerous when it eventually made it on stage, nothing was demanded of my body that it wasn't designed to do. The body can move in so many ways; its design is pretty incredible. Dancing will always push physical limits, but with this facility there are all kinds of ways to produce and release power if you know it well enough. Look at what stunt men do.

I learnt a lot about phrasing from playing the guitar. Take a simple blues riff; you can play it in a million different ways. But then you get someone who plays it in a way that is unique and it changes the evolution of music. Jimi Hendrix did this. I can hear a traditional blues riff he played and think 'I know the notes he's playing, but how the hell did he make it sing like that...?' This is true also with actors – the way they emphasise a word or line in a script can change its whole meaning, sometimes the meaning of a whole play or film. It is the same with phrases in dance. You have to experiment and be wise, recognise the possibilities and what the effect of implementing them will be. Some great choreographers work in a particular established style but it is the *way* they use that style that gives them a voice.

How long should a phrase be? I know when a phrase is a phrase; it speaks to me. You might not want punctuation – you might want a continuous flow – but always consider it even if you believe that we shouldn't think in terms of phrasing at all and that it is all just a continuous line but if I just go on and on in this sentence without phrasing and punctuation after a while you'll get lost and what I'm saying won't be going in especially if I repeat myself too much... But, read *Last Exit to Brooklyn*; some passages don't have any punctuation for pages, and they are brilliant. And they *do* have phrasing in that they have rhythm. It requires a combination of many elements to establish a phrase. Even if music is continuous (I'm not talking about a drone) you will hear phrases within it. Even if you want to make a continuous stream maybe establish where you think phrases are within it. Clarify them and I think you won't lose the effect you want. In fact you will have improved it. Everything has phrasing. Listen to a birdcall, the gunning of a car engine. Listen to an actor reel off some fast text, but listen out for the phrasing. Normally you won't be thinking about this because these decisions will be delivering what the actor is trying to say – the information and the emotion. Phrasing is like structure, a tool for manipulating an audience.

A little more about 'clutter'. I have been writing for over twenty years. I wrote three novels and I threw them all in the bin (I've written books since then that I haven't thrown in the bin), but those years of study were not a waste of time: learning the craft of communication with words informed my work in choreography. One of many things I learnt was how to remove clutter and how much better the writing is without it. Continually assess this because clutter is very good at hiding itself. It is very easy to over-choreograph; we can get carried away by 'flow' once we've hit on a vocabulary and are producing lots of movement with it. It is one of the most common traps to fall into in dance, especially these days with so many ways to move and some vocabularies that flow relatively easily. Well-crafted work will find a flow, then edit, question, audition, think of musicality, think of how one phrase can perhaps say more than ten. I got caught in this trap quite a few times early on in my career when movement was pouring out of me. I didn't have the knowledge or experience to hold back on it.

After attention to all these details, what are my phrases now? Do I 'feel' they are saying what I want to say, or at least saying *something*? What are they saying to my outside eye? Maybe not what I wanted – wait, maybe they are but not how I expected. I was trying to capture something – have I done that? Is this *really* what I want to say? Am I already going back to my preparation – characters, narrative, music, structure, and questioning it? Now the process is really kicking off and the meter is running. All these questions need to be tackled now. I could be heading on a path I didn't foresee.

The dancers and I give phrases names: 'Scarecrows', 'The Spanish', 'Chickens', 'Trojans', 'Gypsy'; all kinds of things. Nowadays we film a phrase when we feel we are capturing it so that nothing is lost (this also prevents arguments when we come back to them). At first I am obsessed with what *I* am doing, finding, then I add the element of the artists learning the phrases with me because that is going to alter everything. Dancers are not machines, and isn't that great? I always say my material is like a script you give to an actor. I will be specific about all aspects of the script – the details and the big picture, but it will be passed on to them for their interpretation and they will take it forward, and eventually I will give it to them. They will own it as they will own their character, their place in the work.

I won't be finished with my initial work on a single phrase until I know every detail of it and have several phrases in the same vein. And then myself and the dancers will leave them be. Tomorrow they will have settled a little in everyone's bodies, and we'll start working on them again. I'll start making some other phrases. Something completely different and go through all the same processes again. All this material goes in the 'choreography bank'. Tonnes of it. The last session I did with my company we did this every day for two weeks straight. We had about forty minutes worth of material by the end, some of it already transposed, some thrown together into sequences, some tried with music, some duets sketched out. Importantly, I've started my creative choreographic process in the studio, begun the exploration of different choreographic vocabulary that might go into the production. At this time everything is scattered in one's mind. This is normal. Have faith that this hard work is all worthwhile and something will form out of the chaos.

Right at the beginning of the rehearsal process I am considering my structure. I want to paint it in gradually as I go along, a bit here, a bit there, so I am growing an initial picture early in the process. I will want to have a very rough first draft, even if everyone else is reeling around, by roughly three to fours weeks into rehearsals, if not before. Even if I work on raw material for most of the first days I'll want an image, a blocking-out of something to take home to think about, even if it is very simple. In choreographic terms my structure will have solos, duets, trios, group sections, all kinds of combinations that begin as blank spaces in my timeline waiting to be filled in. Choreography takes longer than blocking out a basic dramatic line for a scene, or an image, so I'll begin to choreograph these sections, sometimes starting from scratch, sometimes using material from the choreography bank, sometimes just informed by it or a combination of everything. I will be considering all I have written about so far in this book as I do this, but, as always, I will lead with instinct and intuition.

CHOREOGRAPHING TO MUSIC

I mentioned when writing about phrasing that I sometimes start without music, even when I have music in mind. Music is a very powerful ingredient and is to be used with awareness and care. It changes everything, stabs our subconscious with association and emotion. It will completely alter how your work is perceived.

If your aim is to tackle a very powerful piece of music, you may want to hold off playing it immediately in the studio. If you are going to match this music it will take time. Your movement material will need time to grow. If you play the music immediately it can overpower what you are doing, lead you too much, and it can also be disheartening – you may think – I'll never be able to accomplish this. I suggest you know your music well, then begin making material with it playing in your head. This also avoids the dancers dancing to it too much when they should be exploring the musicality of a movement phrase in its own right.

Sometimes I choreograph strictly to the structure of a piece of music, sometimes only to the essence of it – what it brings up intuitively, or at times I work consciously against it, make my own structure and place it on top, and see what happens. I am prepared to change music and have several pieces in mind for one section/scene. So often the music I end up using is a million miles away from what I originally had in mind. Some music is just there to inspire a particular movement identity that marries with my subject matter. I can take just that movement and put it in my phrases but with different music. The results of this can be very interesting and help avoid doing the obvious.

Sometimes I play music in the background as I'm working, let it seep into what I'm choreographing, like subliminal flavours, maybe just giving me a different accent, impulse, emotion. This can get too much sometimes, so switch it off, listen to silence – that's good too. I'm careful with music with words. Words can be misleading. They push to the front of the queue and can distract an audience. A level of ambiguity in words can marry well, but if they are too specific – will the audience just think you are imitating them?

Sound is everywhere. When I'm in France I listen to the cicadas, whose sound inspires ideas of place, atmosphere and movement. Environments

have their own distinctive sounds just as they have their own scents. Be aware of theses – sometimes they are so present we can miss them. It is the same as not seeing all the movement going on around us.

SPACE

The stage is your canvas. There are things to consider but no rules about how it should be used. I *know* my spacing, the picture is already in my head, and I only consider it objectively once the initial image has been created, and then only to a point – usually when something doesn't feel quite right, could be improved or made clearer. At each venue I space everything by inches, tweaking, until the picture rests right on a stage. For the purpose of this book I have to think about the elements that dictate to me when I am doing all this. The pictures in my mind's eye are framed like photography. Now I realise that I think in widescreen. I think from landscape to close-up and everything in-between. I see it like cinema. How do you create a close up in theatre, space things so it alters the perception of a space? How do you draw the audience to look at that close-up shot? And how does this work in the round? When I think about work in this format I suspect I don't think in widescreen, cinema anymore, so my approach to space changes and I have to reassess everything. When a picture you thought could only work one way has to be delivered differently, you realise it can work in so many different ways. When I envisage work in the round my mind's eye is slowly moving, circling the work.

Everything will alter a viewer's perception of space, even temperature and smell. Think about environments, places. Theatres, warehouses, galleries, shopping malls, corridors, graveyards, stadiums – you name it – they all bring their identity into play. Some theatres are black boxes, you 'make your own space' with light and sets and the people in it. This is the closest you get to a blank canvas. Sometimes this is great, sometimes not. Sometimes the inspiration for a work can be the space itself. I like old theatres because they have history and tradition that can marry with what I am putting in them. These spaces have mystery and ghosts.

Where you put a body in a space will change the perception of the space around it. Putting a dancer in an upstage corner facing front will make you perceive the space differently than if you put them in the same place but facing the back wall. Notice a performer's eyes. If they look up the audience will subconsciously consider the space above them. The sound of thunder, a dancer looks up – the audience will picture the sky, not the roof of the building. So sound also manipulates the perception of space. In movies you imagine a whole world out there just because there is the sound of it, when in fact it has been shot in a studio. Anything you put in the performance space will alter the perception of it. Put in a wardrobe and the viewer will add that to their imagination of what the space is. Put in a square of astroturf – will the viewer perceive an idea of what the space represents rather that being based on realism? Is your space based on something literal or is it abstract, or something in-between? Draw a chalk circle on the floor. You have divided the space. What happens if you stand inside or outside the circle? If you are

using projection or monitors or any form of new media this creates portals to other spaces within your space. Now that the internet is everywhere a room is not a room anymore; there are doors within that room going to other worlds.

Here is an example of space in conjunction with other elements, other decisions. The performers have been placed in different spaces with their backs to each other. The light has been used to accentuate the separation – an indoor light and a blue square – a colder space. Now the other elements: the phone, the eye make up smeared down the character in the foreground's face, the black veil over the head of the character in the background. In this scene when the woman picks up the phone the background character plays a tiny music box. It's difficult to get all the connotations of this photograph when disconnected from the rest of the production, but this is Iphigénie calling her mother to tell her that she is dead. Now, the audience might not get this reference but they might get *something,* something that connects with their personal experience or their fears. When you listen to the lyrics of your favourite song, do you really know what the words mean or does it only matter that they mean something to you? (Incidentally this production was in the round. You won't know this because the framing of this picture has narrowed your perception of space by what it has omitted). Something inside me tells me very early on if a piece I am thinking about is going to be set in the round. I trust this 'voice'. Why is circus in the round? Greek Tragedy? Spacing in the round is ritual.

Every exit or entrance to or from the stage leads somewhere within the world you have created on the stage. Where do these performers go? We create illusions. Anyone who visited the *Dracula* set backstage couldn't believe how cramped it was, because of all the work that went into making the audience fill in the space beyond with their imagination.

You also might want to consider an element similarly used in movement: repetition. The markers, islands you plant in the viewer. A cop and the wooden box he sits on, a shotgun on his lap, always downstage stage left. The entire stage behind belongs to him and he guards it from anyone getting in or out. If he returns to this place, we are returned to this environment, this space. We have a marker that makes us consider what has gone before and if things have changed since we last visited this space. Or has no time passed? Is this all happening in the cop's mind, or is it on a loop? A spacing decision has gone into setting this up. You can do this in a literal or abstract way. You can then add all kinds of decisions. What happens if someone repeats an earlier sequence but in another part of the space?

In *Dracula* every scene was set up like a painting: the coffins at the beginning, the chaise longues in the parlour, Lucy's bed, Lucy's grave, Dracula's dinner table. I didn't change any of the spacing from the original pictures in my mind apart from experimenting with the positioning of the carriage, and even then I returned to my original picture. Obviously, there are places on stage that hold more power than others, but I don't think about that too much either – Dracula starts the production dead centre stage. I knew that was how I wanted to introduce him – here he is, and he is in control (for now). But I only realised these reasons when I stood him there. It was also different from the usual way the character of Dracula is introduced – as a sinister presence in the darkness often not appearing until much later on.

Dancers traveling on different diagonals always means different things to me, and the meaning changes with each piece. A pattern emerges within a piece, and I tend to set myself rules with it. I think pathways that establish themselves add clarity.

The layout of a room you like. How you arrange your work on a desk so you can concentrate better. Nothing in the world exists without spacing. On stage you choose the elements to put into a space and the world outside will inform you on this. Without realising you've been absorbing spacing all your life, just as you have structure, movement, language. Spacing begins in the subconscious, like ideas. Execute it and evaluate it later to learn what you already know.

REPETITION

I suspect I'm doing a lot of this in writing this book. Repetition is a powerful tool used all the time in dance and I've touched on its use in earlier chapters. Some pieces use repetition as a theme in the way that some music does, building themes that slowly evolve from patterns. You can repeat single movements, phrases, whole sections – it is entirely up to you. You can make repeats intentionally obvious, or you can use them more subtly, you can suggest them, give glimpses of them then whip them away so the viewer thinks *Have I seen that before? When?* and something in their subconscious relays them back to an earlier point, something important that you want them to remember.

I use repetition in structure intuitively, especially in duets. I know when I need just that one move, that one phrase to come back, then move on, or if I need to transpose that phrase to the floor, say, so it is a repeat but subliminal, recognisable even though the audience doesn't know it is a form of repeat. Pausing can be repetition, a character that always takes a little more time to make a decision reestablishes a trait of that person. I did this with Odysseus lighting a cigarette, reminiscent of old Westerns, as a repeated motif. It set up that he was about to make a choice that might be reckless, or ruthless, or clever, or for love. But it also set up that he was contemplating that at times we have no choice.

The wolves at the beginning of *Dracula* use movement that reoccurs in other sections, a little different but recognisable; the action, the characters and the stories have moved on, but the nature of the beast is still there. Say a character does a solo at the beginning of a work. He is young, alive. At the end he repeats that solo, but he dances it as if broken or old. Time has passed, the repetition suggests memory or an attempt to recapture something, or that an old feeling still resides inside. The word 'echoes' comes to mind when I think of this.

Say you begin a work with a phrase. The audience doesn't 'get' the phrase. It is perhaps a little obscure. But then at the end of the piece the phrase is repeated, and because of everything else that has occurred in-between you now feel you understand what that phrase is. A jigsaw has been made.

What else is repetition? The impulse of the physical identify you have established with the choreography for a section or scene. A problem with some pieces is they repeat a physical identity too much, they can't seem to get out of it so the piece stays on one dynamic level. I reckon pieces need different levels otherwise people zone out. They come back after a few minutes but they haven't really missed anything.

We repeat ourselves all the time. It is part of who we are. We get bored of ourselves, we can get stuck in loops without realising. This is one of the main challenges in life – can you get yourself out of your own loops? If you can do it in life maybe you can identify the loops in your work and get out of those too – or not, if you are still delving deeper into whatever your loop is. Then I guess it isn't really a loop – you're not stuck in it. I get bored of myself – I always return to similar things but I drive them on. This is what repetition is about; establishing, learning and moving on. That's what kids do, they repeat the same games again and again because their brains are developing, as are their motor skills. I've already written about this in relation to stories. Kids say *read that bit again* because they are logging it in their brains – markers – islands…

Dance training is all about repetition. I wonder if that has subliminally threaded itself into our sequences. I have at times followed musical scores to the letter, repeating themes when they do. Songs do this really simply but more complex music can be much more interesting in its use of repetition, development and transposition. I guess this is what I try to do.

TRANSPOSITION AND RETROGRADE

I have used these terms already. I didn't start choreographing using either of these – it never occurred to me. I was too busy finding the beginnings of my movement language and had plenty to get on with. You don't have to use these tools, and often I don't, but transposition and retrograde are great ways to explore the further potential of movement; they clarify your choreographic elements and 'rules' of ingredients for a section/scene, and can contribute to your structural clarity. They contain repetition, but with stealth; just as a piece of music will repeat a section but develop it. They are great things to have as part of your repetition toolkit.

As choreographers there will come times when we want to break out of our movement patterns. We can feel that we are stuck, repeating ourselves. Simply transposing a floor phrase to a standing phrase, or vice versa, can force us out of our natural movement patterns, and the results can be a catalyst for the beginnings of a different movement vocabulary. Retrograde will also do this, while really testing and training one's coordination. Be disciplined and accurate with transposition and retrograde (some moves are impossible), be patient and meticulous – in retrograde reverse not only the movement but also the accents, like a film run backwards. Then don't be strict, explore further what you have found.

TO COUNT OR NOT TO COUNT

When I first listen to music I don't analyse the counts, and I'd say this is true of 99% of people. For me counting is purely a practical tool and I will use it to pull a piece of dance together. I don't set dance to counts if I don't have to. Some music is very difficult to count and sometimes I won't count it 'right', but will set counts that work for the dancers. I write counts down and I will check and recheck them; getting them wrong will waste time in rehearsals. With trickier music I will work with my company on the counts, comparing my version with theirs.

Dancers will then take on the responsibility, they will have written the counts down and will lead on this while I work on other things. This is partly because some of my dancers are very good at counts, better than I am, and remembering them myself is no longer the priority – they are the ones who are going to have to dance to them, and it was the same for me when I was a dancer. I also don't find counting interesting, so I tend to get distracted with other things, and often forget them after I've set them. I do that with a lot of steps nowadays, too, and I often have to relearn material I've made from dancers, sometimes just after I've made it. I wasn't like this when I was younger. Maybe I am getting old, or I've made so many steps they just drop out of my head.

Use counts by all means. Learn your way of logging them. Get them right, and be specific about setting them. And, if you are better than me, remember them as well.

DANCING IN YOUR OWN WORK

Many choreographers do this. There are reasons for and against dancing in your own productions and at the end of the day it is entirely up to the individual and their relationship with the art form. It may be what interests you, what your passion is; exploring what you do, who you are. I have always found dancing in my own work tricky because I can only maintain an outside eye to a certain point. Sure, I can video stuff, but it isn't the same. A director needs to be watching what is going on and I can't do that as well if I am in the work and concentrating on what I am doing.

However, the more you dance and perform the more you are going to learn. There have been many times when I have danced in my own work, sometimes out of necessity but, more importantly, at times when I knew I was losing touch with something and needed to get back in the game. As your vocabulary grows and changes, if you are to go on stage and perform it you are going to have to go through the long and detailed process of really learning what it is. This can only be good. One way that this has worked for me is dancing in something I have already made; something tried and tested and approved by myself. In these situations I have trusted other dancers to help with my outside eye so I could become that dancer again.

DUETS/PARTNER WORK

Just as in life, there are so many different ways to have contact with another human being, and as a dancer and a dance-maker you never stop exploring this. I have made many duets, they can be a communication that transcends words and are probably what I enjoyed most as a dancer, as well as a choreographer.

Let's take it as read that everything I have written about with regards to phrasing applies to any material you are making, whether that's solos, duets, trios, or large group sections – they all get the same attention to detail. Below are some duets I choreographed with notes on how I approached them, and how material from several duets in a single work can influence each other and serve the choreographic development and structure underpinning a production:

Helen (1996)

'Sonata for solo violin', Béla Bartók

First section of a 35-minute duet based on the seduction and abduction of Helen of Troy, ending with the death of Paris.

The first section of this duet was choreographed to the first movement of Bartók's incredible sonata, and dealt with the initial seduction of Helen by Paris. I went through every phrase of this score and marked it out according to what I thought it was doing technically, and choreographed every phrase to the phrases of the score. I felt there were two voices in it – a call and answer, a powerful exchange and an instrument (and probably the player) pushed to the limit. I set this section stage right and on two parallel lines that moved up and down stage, each dancer assigned to a line, moving up and down, only crossing over when contact was made between them. The only time these lines were broken away from was a short repeated solo by the man on a diagonal. The structure was full of repeats, variations, repetition, transpositions and retrograde. It was a difficult duet to learn and dance (I know because in later years I danced it). You had to talk it through in your mind as you danced or you would go into the wrong repeat. It is a good example of following a score to the letter and basing one's structure on it. The material was intense and fast, going to and from the floor at speed. The score begins at a high intensity and only gets crazier over its ten minute duration, and I set out to match this. I'd not long been out of Rosas when I made this duet, and what I'd learned there had an influence in the choreographic material.

Made in Heaven (2012)

Suite Bergamasque, L. 75 – 'Clair de Lune', Claude Debussy

I set out to see if I could make a romantic duet to this romantic music without being sentimental, using a traditional vocabulary with an edge of modern movement. I was inspired by Gene Kelly and Debbie Reynolds dancing together in *Singin' in the Rain*, a duet economical and refined in its phrasing and musicality. I didn't break this duet down, study it, I just let it wash through me. Listening to 'Clair de Lune' I saw an image of a couple meeting on a ship in around the 1920s, like ghosts, and I set about making it.

I broke the music down, marking out its themes, repetitions and development. The music teases, swells until it bursts like a wave, which is perhaps where images of the sea came to me. I started by making phrases that the couple did in unison at the moment when the music was at its biggest swell. The material was fast and at times almost like tap dancing, but there was no tap in there. The actual partnering work I made second. This was a traditional duet with a modern twist, but made traditionally – no transpositions or retrograde, just old-fashioned steps, led by the music in movement and structure.

The structure, in very simple terms:

A series of duet phrases punctuated with 'pictures' – an extension in second; the woman in a back bend, the man supporting and promenading her; other promenades – a theme that emerged. The first musical phrases are a long build rising high, then deepening. I echoed this with the movement and the relationship.

A new section of the music – with a more 'dancey' feel – falling down a hill, joy, being swept away. I started this section with two solo phrases for the woman, followed by the man joining her for several phrases in unison (the first section I made). This section culminates to a gentle, intimate conclusion as the couple come together for another promenade, their feet in the sand on a beach as the man turns her.

There is then a slow choreographic recapitulation as the first melody returns. I used elements of repetition, combining the phrases of the first section and adding alterations. The couple have already danced together, they have a relationship and the repeats are like memories – this was what I felt when I heard the music. There is a feeling of nostalgia, that perhaps this is all memory from a time now gone. This element was a key to where this duet fitted into *Made in Heaven*. The second theme of the music then repeats, and the woman repeats the two phrases of her solo. The couple join again and end as they started – the woman stood facing the audience, the man a little way behind her, as if they have walked out of an old photograph and are standing on the deck of a ship in the moonlight.

This age of perceived innocence, an almost Adam and Eve theme, ended up as the opening to *Made in Heaven*. When the woman returned later her dress was old and torn; at other times she became a mermaid.

'Baby Says', The Kills

Another duet from *Made in Heaven*, completely different in style, approach and music.

The material for this duet was floor transpositions from two other scenes. The man's material came from choreography to another track called 'Illinois Blues' by Skip James (but I think even this material came from elsewhere, made to Ligeti perhaps – I can't remember) and the woman's material came from another scene choreographed to 'Pots and Pans', by The Kills.

My first inspiration for 'Baby Says' was a particular lift I always knew would be at the midpoint in the duet. The image of the prairie girl being swung around by the man was the picture I wanted imprint on the audience, and I structured the other material around this point. I made this duet very fast, the dancers exploring the combining of their separate transpositions, their accents communicating, the choreography getting hooked and sucked together. Another repeated theme – a kind of shaking/shimmer the girl did. And in ever pause between the phrases there was a picture between the couple that told a story. The structure also included retrograde.

Second Coming (2015) made for Ballet Black

'Cello Concerto in E Minor', Op.85 I.Adagio, Edward Elgar

A classic example of picking a very powerful and well-known piece of music. This, and the subject matter – a duet for Jesus Christ and Mary Magdalene – made this duet pretty ambitious; I wasn't sure if I could match the music and it also was *en pointe*, something I wasn't sure would work. I was choreographing in the classical technique, but trying to transcend it, do it my way. It took many drafts of each phrase to get to a stage when the material began to match the music.

I knew the structure of the music but worked without it, making phrases, meetings, conversations between the couple. I made these strong in their own right and put them with the phrases of the music, then changed and re-choreographed them again and again. The duet featured a female dancer who was very strong on *en pointe* and a male dancer who could do some incredible lifts. I utilised these qualities. It is really important to choreograph on the dancers before you, challenge them, but acknowledge what they can do. It took a long time for me to find how to use pointe work in a way that was mine and made sense to me, and first I had to get my style of movement into dancers that had never done it before. I knew I had to do this first so they could move on to what they did well but with physical information from me changing the approach. All these things were a challenge on both sides. I told myself that if I couldn't take advantage of working with a dancer this strong *en pointe* and find my way to creating something powerful, then I would have failed as a choreographer. I saw it through. It took time, but sometimes this is what it takes – faith and patience pay off.

Medea (2011) created for Bern Ballet

'Stick Figures: 6 Guitars and 2 Players', Fred Frith

The duet depicted the death of Creon and his daughter Glauce. Glauce is dead, poisoned and mutilated by Medea. Her father Creon cradles her in his arms, the poison infects him and he is also killed. Or does his grief consume him? The music for this section was powerful and incited movement, but without a clear structure to pin anything to, so I created my own structure. I set the duet centre stage. I choreographed the material from scratch – as in there were no transpositions of other phrases from elsewhere in the piece. It was all floor work. Glauce was dead, manipulated by Creon like a rag doll. She dropped her weight all over him as he desperately tried to hold on to her, push her up towards the Gods as if trying to bring her back to life but also with movement of trauma and grief. The structure was very simple: a 'going phrase' (a phrase without any retrograde in it) with a hint of the conclusion; a separation – two solos on their knees danced simultaneous and transposed from the material of the duet work; the couple coming together again, reversing the original duet, but faster, and ended with the conclusion in full – Glauce on top of Creon, crushing him with her death, thrown upwards towards the heavens only to crash down until Creon is exhausted and consumed. From the retrograde section a chorus also danced material taken from Creon's movement, like an echo, or shockwaves of his grief. The chorus then dragged both the bodies away.

I made this duet in about two to three hours. And it was all made gently.

Duets from *Dracula* (2013)

These four duets from *Dracula* have a connection in choreographic and dramatic material.

Chorale Prelude: 'Ich ruf' zu dir, Herr Jesu Christ', Johann Sebastian Bach, played by Vladimir Horowitz

This was the opening duet for Mina Murray and Jonathan Harker. One of the first phrases I made for *Dracula* was Mina's first movements in this duet. Jonathan's movement was a gentle transposition of the wolves and gypsy material. The transposed Jonathan material was threaded together with Mina's original material, and alongside this I developed a baroque/classical vocabulary. The couple dance in a Victorian garden, after which Jonathan sets off on his travels to Transylvania. There are elements of gentle tenderness, true love, innocence, playfulness, social etiquette, romance, quiet bravery. The contact between the couple is completely different to that of Creon and Glauce. They are so in love that the slightest touch travels through them. Mina's heart flutters. The theme of contact punctuates the structure. The first move is Jonathan placing his hand on Mina's shoulders. She closes her eyes and smiles, lets Jonathan guide her, trusting him in a gentle game they are playing. But it is more than a game: Mina is completely trusting Jonathan in *everything*, and the feeling is blissful. Their relationship is set up from this first move, but also by the physicality of how they dance together. The couple live in a time and society in which touching would be mostly the shake or possibly kiss of a hand, but these two are going beyond this, and the excitement and joy of that is there, though kept in check, restrained, hanging on to that beautiful flowering moment. This is what the magic of *Dracula* is very much about – the tease. Deep down we know that the women of Dracula are going to go from one extreme to another.

The music has subtle melodies and a structure that is hard to pin down when simply listening to it. The choreography responded to each suggestion the music gave, answering, leading, giving space. I like music with space in it, I can add to it, play with it. There is a strong call and answer in the music's structure; the phrases are wonderful, the way they bleed into one another, never predictable. You feel you are getting repeats but they are never quite the same. I instinctively did this with the choreography – there is only one move halfway through that is clearly repeated at the end of the duet. All other repeats are alterations, combinations and development. In terms of spacing the duet worked on a zigzag diagonal that the couple travelled along, beginning upstage and ending downstage on a journey they took together.

Allegory III: String Quartet & Electric Guitar, 'For Irvine Arditti', Fred Frith

Mina and Jonathan's next duet takes place in the second act, after Jonathan has returned from his terrible experiences at the hands of the Count. Mina and Jonathan are married, but they are both scarred by what has happened. Jonathan is numb, ill, his mind plagued by Dracula, who exists inside him, leading him to doubt his own sanity. Mina wants to take care of him, but already she can feel the presence of the vampire. Is it Dracula or Jonathan's own dark animal that he feels inside himself? The duet is punctuated by images of Dracula behind the wrought iron bars of the set, in the shadows, with his vampire brides. They fade in and out representing the images in Jonathan's mind as he and Mina return home to their wedding bed. The material is original, combined with floor transpositions of material from their first duet, as if trying to recapture what they had; but it is interrupted, their touch at times clumsy or even violent. There is a sexual tension, a need between them, and it is sad and desperate. As with their first duet, the scene is set dramatically before it moves into dance, beginning with Mina leading Jonathan home from their wedding. She takes care of him, undresses him, before symbolically letting her hair down. Their initial contact in the dance is initiated by Jonathan who puts his hand on Mina's leg, and she reciprocates by putting her hand on his. It is different, intimate.

The music of this duet is incredibly evocative and I love it the more and more I listen to it. It combines strings with other sounds (somewhere a bird is singing). It suggests many emotions. Somehow it creates a feeling of an insane asylum and this marries with the mental state of many of the protagonists of *Dracula* and much of the book that is set in a Victorian asylum; a theme I developed with the vampire brides – a suggestion of fallen women. Mina's material is mixed with that of the vampire brides, suggesting she is finding a connection with this side of herself, or is it the way Jonathan perceives her after his encounter with the vampires who nearly destroyed him? It is also a suggestion of Mina's metamorphosis that is to come.

The duet moves simply from one side of the stage to the other. There are no choreographic repeats, but times when Jonathan pulls away from Mina only to return to her. The tension of the duet gradually increases until they find each other at the end; there is not a resolution in hope to the future of their relationship, but the love is in there somewhere. It is tragic where they are now compared to where they they began.

'Requiem Lacrimosa', Alfred Schnittke

Mina Harker has two duets with Dracula. The first takes place after she has heard of the death of her best friend Lucy, and has been left alone by the men who have gone out searching for the Count (one of the crazy decisions the men of *Dracula* make). The Count comes to claim her, but as the duet develops Mina grows in strength and there is a turning point at which the power shifts. The choreography is original – no transpositions of other sections – and I made it in about forty minutes (it just happens like that, sometimes). The biting and drinking is a theme, and the only repetition, although it is done differently each time, and at the end Mina bites and tries to drink from Dracula. Again, this duet begins with a simple initial touch. Mina has her back to the Count, but senses him behind her (her first duet with Jonathan begins this way but the feel is completely different). The Count touches her face – something a Victorian gentleman would never do, or not in such a claiming manner – then he bites her. She is shocked, lifted from her knees. Only when he lets her down does she turn to face him and sees him for the first time (more than an hour into the production).

The phrases of the duet have pauses between them, unlike Mina's first duet with Jonathan in which each phrase bled into the next. There are moments of heavy tension and change between Dracula and Mina in these pauses, things considered, changes that need time to settle after each movement encounter between them. Some of the material has a classical vocabulary, and is very simple, like the music – refined elements explored to their potential in terms of power. Dracula is an animal, is all over her, their contact rough. Mina is lifted and manipulated but stands her ground, becoming gradually more empowered. Then she turns on him and the power shifts.

'Lancashire Pipes', Vittorio Ghielmi & Luca Pianca

Dracula ends with a last duet between Mina and Dracula. I left the making of this duet until last, after the rest of the production was made. It took me a while to decide on the conclusion; as I mentioned in an earlier chapter, I didn't have a definitive one in my prewritten structure because I wanted to see what was going on in the performers before I made that decision. I also felt that the ending of the novel was unsatisfactory to me, and that I had to draw my own conclusions.

Mina dances with Dracula until the sun rises and destroys him. But it was their attitudes that took time to define – who were they now? For Dracula there was a feeling of resistance and then letting go. A redemption, a fleeting moment of feeling what it is to be truly alive, not a walking deadman without a soul. And who is Mina at the end – half vampire? The future?

The material combined elements of every section of the production: the Count's solo, the classical baroque element, wolves, gypsie, the fight scene, the previous duet between them, and a development of this material including a jumping section. There is an 'island' in the middle of the duet (I wrote about 'islands' in my chapter on structure); the couple have met, danced, but now Mina begins to lead Dracula towards a rising sun and he is afraid. The dance continues but now she leads him on to his death.

The music has many elements to it, many suggestions of styles, but they are not specific; it has a strange folk sound, and something almost medieval.

We changed the ending a little when we remounted the production. Originally Mina stood over Dracula as he lay down and died. This was strong and harsh. In the later version this changed to her kneeling and putting her hand on his head as he died – a gesture not quite sentimental but perhaps a connection, an understanding and union between them. Many things.

I hope that in going through these examples it is clear how different structures and approaches to choreography, drama, character, music, and narrative, all combine to create something. Every one of these duets has its own physical identity and choreographic language, and their creation is a combination of intuitive and objective decisions.

GROUP SECTIONS

A group of dancers is a powerful thing. Group sections are markers in a production, showing people coming together – the ballroom scene, the battle scene, the courtroom; a crowd, a ritual; a bullfight, a social dance, a wedding, a funeral, an angry mob, a lynching, a crime scene. They don't have to have any dramatic meaning; they can be about structure, orchestration, musicality. They can be used just to enhance your work. It is liberating in dance that an audience won't necessarily need to 'know' a meaning for a group section; they will accept whatever you throw at them and are often happy to just enjoy it. All this is at your disposal, and you can mix it all up.

Is a group formed of individuals, are they collective, or are they a representation of the subconscious of an individual? Are they commenting on the action like a Greek chorus, or are they part of it? Do they know the audience is watching? Or can they be a combination all these things?

Here are a few examples of group scenes and how I approached them. And within these I'm going to write a little about cannon and unison.

Gypsy Dance, *Dracula*

'Kozbunarsko Xoro' (The Wedding procession). Trifon Trifonov & Stanimaka

Traditional group dances can be very specific and intricate. I went all round the houses making the 'gypsy' dance for Dracula. At first I thought I wanted the gypsies to be wild, and the music I chose had a crazy and very physical element to it. But something wasn't working. I looked up traditional Eastern European folk dances. I saw the care and attention to detail, the specific nature of executing a vocabulary. I saw complete dances taking place in restaurants in traditional costume. There was sometimes an almost doll-like quality to the dancers, and I realised I had seen this quality in my mind when listening to the music. It was as if the dancers had stepped out of a painting.

The gypsies in *Dracula* still had their wild moments in their dance, but they also had their traditions and respect for these traditions. Jonathan Harker was experiencing their world, they were introducing and involving him in it. They appeared rugged and wayward but then once he got to know them he felt comfortable and was released by the increased speed and celebration of the dance. At the end he felt drunk and happy until he informed the gypsies he was going to visit Castle Dracula and suddenly realised he didn't know them at all; that he was in a foreign world. The enjoyment of the dance had led him into a false sense of security. I wanted it to be the same for the audience – I wanted them to forget they were watching *Dracula* and that something bad was going to happen.

I used unison in this dance. Unison is the simplest of tools that will increase the power of what you are doing. Group dances often involve unison but I avoid using it all the time because it is almost *too* easy; I use it when I feel it makes dramatic or ritual sense. Many traditional dances use it. My gypsy dance had several sections. It began with a solo gypsy woman introducing the material, a vocabulary of made up 'folk' steps incorporating ballet but danced very differently. The woman was enticing Jonathan to get up and dance with her and the other women joined, repeating a variation of these steps. The men joined and everyone began to dance in partners, Jonathan in the middle with the solo gypsy woman. The speed increased until the dance broke off into a wilder section – the men dancing together, answered by the women and then the men again. Now the dance became a series of patterns. One of my dancers knew traditional Welsh folk dance and we used this, including a rhythmical step that bounced along with the music, keeping the pace going and making it celebratory. The dancers wound in and out of each other, then returned to their partners, repeating a combination of the original material but now very fast and into a traditional big finish.

The dance was set to complex counts, I spent a long time with the dancers working out what we thought the counts were until we all agreed on one version.

Chorus Dance, *Medea*

'Stick Figures. 6 Guitars and 2 Players', Fred Frith

I've used this as an example of how you can make a very simple structure effective. This was group section for a chorus of fourteen dancers. I made a series of phrases, then divided the dancers into two groups and laid the phrases on top of each other with each group dancing them in a different order. Each group kept in unison as they sliced through gaps between one another. The dancers were strict about their phrasing, and pauses between and punctuation within each phrase gave this section clarity. There was a moment in the middle when one group paused for longer and waited for the other group to catch up. This felt like a halfway breath, before it all kicked off again. The dancers in this work had a strong classical technique. There were a lot of jumps in the phrases. My advice about jumping – don't avoid it. There is a whole vocabulary of jumping to be explored.

Maenads and Dionysus dance, *Sea of Bones*

'Covered in Punk's Blood', Volumes 9&10, The Desert Sessions

We called this section 'chickens' because you felt like a headless chicken doing it and afterwards like you had whiplash. But once the movement really got into your body it felt fine and didn't hurt so much. The movement was a feeling of the lightning power of the god Dionysus striking into the body, dancers crashing all over the place. I used cannon, but not with a regular rhythm, more like scattered echoes going back and forth. In terms of floor patterns, the section above from Medea worked very much with zigzagging between groups, but 'Chickens' had a feeling of a magnet centre stage – the dancers pulling away from it and being dragged back. 'Chickens' is also an example of the evolution of a section through a working process. It began life as a seven-minute opening scene to a Sonic Youth track. We worked and worked the material, then I thought I could say it all in one minute, and changed the music. We toured *Sea of Bones* with this section like this but I was never convinced I'd solved it. When we re-toured the production I changed the music again, re-choreographed it, and developed the material. I re-spaced and structured it differently and merged it with the scene afterwards which had been a solo for a man. So now the male dancer danced among the females. This section was now one minute forty seconds. It is interesting that the material also grew in strength over the year that we did this piece. So as the dancers got better at it, I could take it forward.

Maenads' dance, Sea of Bones

'No Wow', The Kills

This section was about life. It was empowering, and in a way it was the reward for all the hard work that went into the making of *Sea of Bones*. It was a ritual the audience witnessed, and being watched was part of the ritual. The dancers had pride and celebrated their power, their prime, being taken by it. Their scars were for all to see and this was part of the celebration – getting knocked down, but being able to take it and stand again. They were like warriors, becoming stronger through everything they had been through in the piece so far. It pushed and set them up for the last part. It made everything they had been through real – they were the characters in the work but more so they were themselves. They were also one, a strength rising from the power of the group. They did this ritual and then dived back into the piece, but at that moment they had stepped out to acknowledge the audience.

The structure and movement was simple and absolutely specific – the accents and articulation refined – no clutter. The five women stood in a line facing the audience, their moves rippling along the line like shock waves; twists and turns, crashing into walls, striking back. I listened to the music and saw the main theme of the pumping fists immediately. I also wrote out the structure in one listen, dividing the track into sections which I set to counts. I worked on all the movement elements but didn't put them together – I gave rules to the dancers of which moves they could put in what section, and how many in a sequence before they returned to the main theme of the fists. From these rules the dancers formed their own sequences. As the sections progressed I added movements and the phrases became longer with less stops so the whole piece built in tension and speed.

The 'island' was the theme – coming back to the fists each time, but I developed this, doubling up the speed and ending with the dancers bent forward doing it until they couldn't do it any longer. And there was one wildcard – one dancer did a Brazilian shimmy in the middle.

I hope all I have written about creating movement begins to answer how one goes about forming the choreographic structure underpinning a work. You must look at your structure both as a whole and in sections with an outside eye, but I also find that following the process I have described will find that things begin to instigate their own structure. It is like pieces in a jigsaw slowly coming together. A process has set a chain of events in motion and the work almost seems to be making itself because of a nurturing and attention to detail. It is alive. Hopefully it isn't a monster. But then again – maybe that's what it is supposed to be. I'm often disturbed by what starts to grow before me.

Drama

I have always directed intuitively, whether with actors or dancers, and my process has evolved through a need to achieve something. What I am saying is – I've made it up as I go along. Searching, solving something that isn't working, and producing a vision has formed the basis of my craft. A lot of this comes down to communication, and actors communicate and think about so many things that a dance training simply won't equip you with. I have no 'training' in theatre, yet I cross over into this field all the time, and even took near six years out from my company while I worked more in this area than pure dance. I soak up information, always want to increase my knowledge. It's good to get out of the dance world sometimes. Like any world I guess.

There are so many skilled actors and directors out there, so anything I can contribute must come from who I am and the mix of what I do. I took to communication with actors immediately. I found my approach to making work had a lot naturally in common with their process. But my process also marries with the approach to creation in dance, and in this case I *am* trained in the medium – trusting your instinct, striving into the dark and leaving your mind behind but at the same time maintaining a discipline – accuracy, consistency in hitting a move, a line, timing, spacing… not to say that actors don't do all this, but dance adds something through its nature of its intense physical training. I incorporate this physical discipline in my approach to character and storytelling. I combine discussion, collaboration, with just telling people what to do. Sometimes I sketch out a scene (I don't mean blocking – that's a little different) so I can 'compose it', asking myself all sorts of questions before deciding my picture is right, and only then do I go into explanation and discussion about what it is about. This is because the choreographer in me is creating the drama with all sorts of different tools (everything I am writing about in this book). Dancers will quickly find the physical characteristics of the creature and inhabit it, stylise it. They can be half-acting half-being, and be prepared, at first, to not know what they are doing.

Dance is a very free medium when it comes to narrative – you don't *have* to have 'characters' or to 'tell' the story. So dancers have a lot of

freedom. Choices. They can be a character doing something or they can be themselves and not have to conceal this fact. Often in dance theatre you can be aware that it is the real person not a character you are watching, and this is OK. They are embodying an emotion or state of being, not a character in a story. They can fluctuate between or combine these approaches. The place where everything meets is often where I find myself and what interests me.

In straight theatre actors *will* find themselves in a character but they still have their script. In dance theatre you have your draft of a script, but you can start again. You can decide who is really performing. You can tear up your script and transcend your story because what is happening with the real person is more interesting. I often go through a dilemma when writing cast lists for programmes. I know who a character is based on, but do I want to tell this to the audience? Can't the audience make up their own mind who a character is, or can't they just watch the real person without having to perceive them as playing a character? Is that Zeus or is it just a dancer with Zeus inside of him? Dance theatre is ritual, and the dancers are animals in an arena. I always say the moment you are looking for as a dancer is when you have worked so hard to get something right, you are no longer thinking. You are moving, touching the other. All your training has gone into these fleeting moments. Dance connects with music in this sense; when you see a live music performance you are witnessing a musician as themselves reaching for something. These moments don't happen all the time, and they don't always happen on stage. Some of the best moments I had as a dancer happened in the studio. A time when I thought – I nailed that, I felt it. Though, and this is so common, there are times when you'll be told you did a good performance and you think *did I? I really didn't feel it.*

Very early in my career as a dancer I learnt a harsh lesson. I was playing Faust, and I didn't know any better than to literally go on stage every night and sell my soul to the Devil, lose everything, and die. I completely burnt myself out. Then I realised I had to learn to act. I had to work out what I was doing and recreate this without destroying myself. I've witnessed actors doing this – their technique taking them through. I always try and pick this out when a dancer is doing something great but doesn't know, or know how, they are doing it. Because of their training, once you tell them they can be very consistent about recreating it. Their technique comes in to play.

I find a creature, a trait in a dancer that connects with my subject matter, a character I am exploring, and nurture it in a non-judgemental environment. You have to stumble and your dancer needs to stumble. If you spend too much time edging towards something because you are afraid of falling you can waste a lot of time. Go beyond what you know, you can always come back and say *well that didn't work,* or *yes – but maybe a little less,* or *that was absolutely terrible but I have learnt something that I can take into my next approach to finding whatever it is I am looking for, or think I am looking for.*

Say I have found a creature, but I don't have a 'scene'; just an emotion they are expressing, or a statement they are making. This is when symbolism comes into play. Is there an action that marries with the creature, something the creature can do that symbolises this? I mix this with permission to slide between all these decisions:

The murdered mermaid lying on a silk sea suddenly wakes up. Her tail is gone. She pulls the silk up around herself and walks away. Is this performer still the mermaid or is she her real self? Was she reliving her personal loss of innocence when she had her tail severed? The dancer that leaves the stage – could she be her real self in another time – a performer in a sideshow leaving the stage after the curtain has gone down, a show within a show? What *is* her story? Where is she going – back to a caravan in the dark? This connects with what I have said about finding the archetypal in the everyday. Finding history within ourselves. All things rolled into one with this character. It is my hope the audience feels these things, but can't necessarily pin them down. Maybe they will hold on to a version they can relate to themselves. And this is what I really want because decisions of perception belong to the audience. Notice that these ideas have created a story, a structure, through an exploration of character, symbolism and ritual.

The poster image for *Made in Heaven* epitomises this fluctuating state of being. The prairie girl in the picture is captured crossing over to another side of herself, but it is also the dancer doing this. And in this picture *another* decision has come in to play: This character is acknowledging the viewer.

Another image: harpy-like cowgirls, painted blue, walk out of Hades with severed heads in their hands.

In this case the cowgirls are not acknowledging the audience because the action is directed towards a particular dancer. Some of my creatures are allowed to communicate directly with the audience, some are not. If you do do this, will the audience trust, even though they don't trust, that this creature is going to hold their hand through a journey? It is similar to an actor adding an aside, but more ambiguous because the dancer doesn't speak. In *The Odyssey* the only characters allowed to engage with the audience were the immortals, as they dipped in and out of the action, played with it all. But I also broke the rule – the characters of a Father Christmas scene were allowed to engage the audience, which made the whole experience darkly unhinged. And you certainly didn't trust any of them.

Of course, because these performers are dancers they can cross over into incredible movement that transcends these decisions. There are a million more possibilities. I will never get to the end of it all.

IT'S NOT WHAT YOU SAY, IT'S WHAT YOU DO

On the tube, when no one is speaking, the way people sit, dream, look about them will tell stories. In a café or a pub, watch the conversations, interactions, but turn down the volume. Look at gestures, what people wear, the stories in the history of their faces, their character traits, and always, always the eyes. Now listen to some music or sound through headphones. Now you are making a movie.

Here are a selection of screen grabs from *Dracula*. Here's the conversation. What do you think is going on? When this is in motion you have to get the timing of the movement right, and consider the music. Timing is everything. This scene was directed to Scarlatti's 'Sonata in F Minor, Kk.466, L.118, *andante moderato*'. This contributed to the setting of the Victorian parlour and accentuated the gentle interaction between the characters; the piano playing out petals of conversation, but deeply rooted with emotion. The scene involved movement, light, set, costume, spacing, line, music and acting, but no words. Words would be intrusive; what would they have said that the silent interaction did not? The intention was for the audience to 'hear' a conversation that was personal to them. To have had a personal moment with these characters. To feel what they were feeling.

The vampire brides as street girls, this time interacting with the audience – what are they saying?

What does this say?

Or now this?

Again, now we are crossing into dance territory. This is the interesting bit – where dance and drama meet; pushing people's perceptions between one and the other. (Notice also the symbol in the background.)

TEXT

If you are working with text consider professional actors, writers and directors – it's what they do. I suggest you work in theatre for a while, study scripts and literature, and simply start writing and experimenting with words. Like any craft, there are no shortcuts. People dedicate their whole lives to understanding and working with words, so gain as much knowledge from those that do. You might also want to consider collaborating with a writer, actor or director. Studying a script with actors will inform you how to take words from the page, bring them to life and use them to communicate. Knowing this will make you change how you write – it will demonstrate how lean a script can be but how much you can get out of it. A good scriptwriter will know how to pare it down so it is a gift for an actor. If you are starting out as a choreographer I suggest you don't even consider using text at this stage; learning to choreograph is a meal in itself. That's why you can't train to be an actor and a professional dancer at the same time. It's achievable but it takes a long time and separate periods of concentration.

Text can be dangerous with dance. It tends to jump to the front of the queue in an audience's perception, they will latch onto it quickly and, consciously or subconsciously, apply what they think it is saying to your choreography. It rarely works the other way round, unless perhaps it is abstract or cut up, words used as rhythm, sound, music and not forming coherent sentences. Maybe this levels the playing field. Do you want words with your movement? Why? Do you need them? What about what your movement is saying without them, subtle things that you want an audience to make up their own mind about?

Maybe begin by setting yourself the challenge of limiting yourself to choreography – music, pictures, everything else at your disposal to say what you want to say. Then consider if you need or want to incorporate text, realise it is really a fundamental part of your idea. Treat it like an idea – audition it. When I began working on approaches for *Dracula* I wrote a lot of text, mostly for the asylum scenes in which Renfield, the lunatic, converses with his doctor. I even wrote lyrics for songs that he would bash out on an old piano in a music-hall style before running round his cell chasing birds and catching insects. He was almost narrating some of the through-lines of the production. Eventually I cut these scenes along with the character of Renfield. This, alongside other decisions I was making about the production, saw the use of text shrink until it disappeared altogether. It wasn't needed, would jar with everything else and become a hindrance to the progression of other elements.

Words are powerful but they are a minefield and can be misleading. Ironically we think they are a clear form of communication, but often this is not the case. Ask someone what they think a meaning of a word is and it can be very different to what you think. Just look at different interpretations of holy scripture, or the way politicians use words to confuse us. This is part of why actors sit down at the beginning of a creative process and talk through all the words. They need to come to an understanding of what they all mean, that they are on the same page as much as possible. And of course no one ever agrees on everything.

I've worked with text and movement individually and combined and in many different ways. How I combine these powerful elements depends on my idea or, in the case of working in theatre, sometimes the task a play presents me with. Just like structure, the method is subservient and every idea will initiate a different approach. In *Made in Heaven* the android-like cop spoke lines almost familiar to us from movies, but the lines had a twist to them. The cop knelt down by the dead mermaid and spoke through a walkie-talkie to other cops in other places on the stage (a device to alter the perception of space), reporting on the crime scene while poking the victim with a pen. We know this – turn on the TV any night of the week and a cop or a forensic expert will be leaning over a dead body. I added the sound of driving rain, and the flashing lights of cop cars through the night, and the cops wore windbreakers. The audience has been manipulated into picturing the scene and the text is part of this; they feel they are in a place they know. But the cop says 'The victim's tail has been removed...' she is 'young... beautiful... cause of death: bleeding'. They never say that on CSI.

In the case of this scene from *Made in Heaven* I used a number of elements to create the image, and I used the text to subvert the scene, to tell us a little more about the minds of the protagonists and the strange world they were existing in. Add an element because it contributes to a scene, not because it is saying the same thing as something else. A girl eats an ice cream, and at the same time you have a character say 'I saw a girl eating an ice cream.' You don't need to say that. Why use the line at all? The character could just come in and see the girl. But notice the line again 'I *saw* a girl. This tells us this is in the past. How could I place the two characters in the space with this in mind? My intuition tells me that the character speaking is facing the audience with the ice cream scene playing out behind them, as if through the back of their head. Now, what if I remove the text? Does this staging suggest that the character is seeing this scene *and* that it is in the past? What other elements could help achieve this? Time passing is a constant challenge, how to do it in a way that isn't obvious? They cheat in films all the time – that little caption: *three years earlier.*

Writers deal with all of this. Good writing won't dish it out in obvious ways, it will feed it to you via what the characters do, how they behave, what they want, in all kinds of ways. Like Don Draper looking out of an aeroplane window, the sun rising, the light gradually stroking up his face. A new dawn, a new experience is on its way. He does very little, but there is so much going on. Brilliant. No words, but written by a writer. Good writing is clever.

Like choreography, text is everywhere. Hear it and observe what goes with it. Note all the different ways it is used and know that you can use it in any way you want. Advertising – one line to capture you coupled with an image. Lyrics of a good song – some specific, others obscure, others in-between, and how they marry with their music. Poetry, prose – the million different ways writers use words. Verse, cut-up-technique, stream-of-consciousness. How words and the way they are delivered differ from culture to culture – like traditional dance styles, they represent a society, a speed of thought, how emotion is accepted, or a more cerebral approach to things. Know that you are a product of all this, just as is every artist you work with. You know more about it than you may think, so part of approaching text is becoming aware of what you know.

Most dancers are not trained actors, some have an aptitude for text, others need time. As a performer do you need to 'understand' what you are saying? This is an interesting one. Dancers often go on stage and do as they are told, making instinctive physical sense of what they do, but perhaps never having 'thought' about it. As a dancer, when I was handed some text, I just felt my way through it, instinctively made sense of it like a piece of music. I got what the words meant to me but didn't analyse them. I felt the images and 'spoke' the way the words set those images up. The choreographer I was working with gave me rules, gave me direction, but we never discussed what the text meant. I delivered the text at several points in the production including opening and closing the show. I felt what I needed to do, and that included feeding off what went before and after, complimenting, adding, moving us on and probably many other things. When I use text I mostly do go through its meaning, but there have been times when I've just told someone how I want them to deliver a line, which again is more like giving movement direction.

Language is complicated but we all speak it. I don't consider myself a great writer, but I have just as much right to write as anyone else. I may get it wrong but I work at it, make it better, experiment. Much of what I write never sees the light of day; it is about process and the results will often feed other aspects of the work. Moving words around is like choreography. All art forms use similar tools and methods, so they will inform you; just doing some writing will make you a better choreographer. Writing is far more explored than choreography and there are so many things to learn from those that are good at it. And some writers use choreography/action to communicate their ideas. Here is another example of great screen writing from *Mad Men*:

The episode begins with Pete Campbell trying to fix a dripping tap that is keeping him up in the middle of the night. He goes back to bed having fixed the tap and feeling good about himself, and his wife is impressed. It seems to make them feel good about their marriage. Later on there is a gathering at the couple's home. The tap explodes. Don Draper rolls up his sleeves and fixes it. Everyone thinks Don is great and he looks just great fixing that tap. Pete Campbell will never be Don Draper. The tap represents all the ongoing problems and frustrations in

Pete Campbell's life. As the episode ends Pete is woken once more as the tap begins to leak again. The sound of the drips hitting the sink are like time passing, time running out.

The whole episode is wound around this dripping tap, a simple idea that captures the frustration so many people feel with themselves and their lives. Of course there is dialogue, but no one talks about what the tap represents. It is a great example of a symbolic image incorporated with text. It is from things like this that I learn.

Words are always present in us. Our thoughts speak to us in words, whether we want them to or not. I was always fascinated by the idea of what my children were thinking before they had any language. I'm currently working on my version of *Macbeth* without using spoken word, but the verse – the rhythm, sound, emotion, imagery, meaning – is there, expressed through the choreography, the words lying silently underneath everything.

The creative team

Choose your collaborators with care. An exciting conversation in a pub isn't a great basis for seeing out a whole project with someone. I've spent years searching out artists I want to work with. Those I collaborate with are professionals – they work to deadlines, they understand what is involved, how together you need to be to get something on. They also understand that ideas can be cut and reworked; that this is the process.

Mounting productions for stage can become like factory work. No time to think; just reel out the next one. This isn't the best way for everyone to be creative. I begin discussions with my set, lighting and costume designers way in advance, when I am still searching around, working through all my ideas for a production. They want seeds to plant, just like I do. I won't necessarily expect them to be designing anything yet, just thinking about it. Preparing in advance also gets practicalities on the table – what kind of budget are we working with, how many dancers, which venues, what restrictions? A production manger will already be in play – get yourself a good one.

I'll send out drafts of where I am so far with my structure, including reference material, colours, music, films to look at, books to read – anything I think is influencing me. I will describe the world I am looking to create. Describing design ideas helps clarify what is unspecific in my mind, even when I think it isn't, especially when it comes to costume. Sometimes what I give my costume designer is a detail, a collection of colours, an era. She will take on all the information and work out the essence of what on earth I'm going on about. All these things go in a melting pot and a design will emerge that has influences but an identity of its own. A finished design will have transcended the limits of my knowledge and creativity in this area – I am not a costume designer and the design may have turned everything I thought on its head. My costume designer will be working on the design right up until the end of the rehearsal period and be prepared to make big changes at the last minute as everything comes together.

With set design the picture is generally clearer in my mind than it is for costume, but again the ideas will be transcended by my set designer.

There will often be a large number of locations and set pieces the design will have to incorporate. As the design becomes simpler and simpler, but is achieving everything it needs to, and has a 'look' in its own right, I know we are on the right track. Costume and set works in a kind of relay: I give the information, something comes back, I understand a little more and I give more information, something else will then come back to me. With *Dracula* the set designer and myself came back to each other at the same time saying *it's black, and it's made of wrought iron*. We knew we were there then.

With light it works a little differently. My lighting designer and I have worked together for many years, and he is another one of the first people I go to when dreaming up another piece. Light is an incredibly influential tool on stage. The designer and I talk about the 'look' of a production – what the colour palette will be. With *Dracula* we used words like monochrome. We discussed certain films, things emerging from the dark. We also worked with a cinematic depth of field, the dancers needing to be in very specific places at certain times. I won't see a lighting design until we get to production week. This is why I want everything else sorted before this time. Production week or 'tech', is when all design elements come together. But this is when a lighting designer must have their time to do their job.

There will be others in the creative team. I will often work with a sound designer, especially if I am using my music in a production and we want to blend it into the world. I have worked with composers, but I tend to use a lot of existing music, and I have a theme – a linking of sound and music – to pull everything together. I tend to write this myself because I am very specific about it. I am not a proper musician, but I have enough ability to produce what I want. I'm still working at it. Sometimes I work with puppet-makers. I have also worked with visual artists who have made props and masks. I worked with a magician on *Dracula* and *The Odyssey*. The team will be assembled depending on what the production requires.

You might be thinking that you don't have this team, or the money to put a team like this together, but you may not need it – I didn't start out with all these things in place. The company began with six dancers, all of us unpaid, and one technician. We did everything between us, and it is possible. The core of your work is what you create with your dancers. I still have that rule – whatever I make with the cast should be strong without any of the other elements in place. It should be strong in the studio. I think that is a good starting point. In recent years my productions have become increasingly ambitious and so have their needs. But I learnt about everything to do with running a company and getting a show on from the bottom up, just by doing it and picking up information over the years. I didn't just jump into the position I'm in now. The advantage of this is that I know a lot about what is involved in other people's jobs and what their needs are. And believe me, what we produce now within our relative budgets still requires a knowledge of every trick in the book.

The second stage

I have made material, put together scenes, painted the pictures, and now I have a version of my timeline (it will already have evolved from my original timeline through the creative process). How much you need to flesh out the work, tighten it up to see it clearly, is up to you. I like the work to be already well-rehearsed, not finished, but the details and pace should be prominent and clear, otherwise I'll get distracted by what still needs to be done. Of course it isn't going to be right yet, I just need to know where the production is heading, what its potential is. If it's too messy and the flavours aren't there, I can't think about how everything will fit together.

I now repeat my structuring process, asking all the same questions again, evaluating what I have made, am making. What is my cast making? They are fleshing out their characters, their movement, their journey – the characters that were speaking to me in my head are now living breathing people. And isn't that great? I feel where they are leading me, but keep my outside eye. I still know more than them about the big picture they are a part of. They will go off on tangents, just like I did with my ideas. I might find they are working on the beginnings of another piece. I can always put this information away as a starting point for other things.

I make sure I have all the lines of narrative, character, and choreographic development in place; all the journeys. What is proving to be important, what has a strong identity? It may be something that wasn't in my original structure, or something small that has risen up and obliterated some of the earlier ideas. These moments may be the beginning of transcending my structure and producing my next draft. The whole piece might not be what I thought it was, but something has emerged to tell me what it *really* is about. I identify the catalyst. And while doing all this I can mull over ideas for my ending.

I can make crucial changes at this stage. I cut a lot of material. I completely change music. I swap the order of scenes. I don't hang onto something because it is good material, or is an image I love – if it doesn't fit I lose it. The piece has outgrown it. The longer I put this off the more it will get squeezed out by other things and become a blockage that gets on my nerves, by which time I'll have gone off it anyway. In film editors are often separate from the rest of the process. They have no emotional attachment to the shots they cut up. Their job is to pare it down, make it clear. I edit my production; get rid of clutter, get rid of unnecessary repetition. I look at the 'conversations' between the characters – can I cut a few 'lines', like a writer would with a script. I make it lean. Then I can develop what I am left with. I can feel harsh when I am doing this, but looking back on productions I often see more edits that I could have made, rather than things I shouldn't have lost.

We all get stuck sometimes. Don't think – problems, failures, dead ends. Think challenges, learning curves. Use everything written so far to consider ways forward. Here is an example of a combination of approaches leading to a solution:

In Act Two of *Dracula*, there was a series of heavy scenes: the vicious and relentless destruction of Lucy Westernra, drained by Dracula, then caused more pain by her devoted men, all in love with her, trying and failing to save her; her funeral and then her staking (a second death); followed by a sad wedding between Mina and Jonathan, Jonathan damaged and tortured by his experiences abroad with Dracula, followed by Lucy's men arriving to tell of the horrific deed they have just done… all pretty heavy. And the rest of the story doesn't let up from here on. (*Dracula* has no humour in it, something that I grappled with when writing my adaptation.) I had to work out how to deal with this. The darkness had to be there but the audience would not stay with it if it was unrelenting, if it didn't change tack or communicate it in a different way.

There was also a storytelling challenge at this moment: Jonathan Harker has to realise they are all fighting the same enemy, fill the others in with his own untold story, and tell them where to find the Count. Difficult one without words. The dancer had a solo but it didn't work for me; too much storytelling through movement. I had always anticipated several challenges within this scene and with its connection to the scenes around it, and deliberately decided I would solve this in the studio rather than in advance. Because I'd done my homework I knew that I wanted to solve this with symbolism and, more importantly, a dark humour. I'd had humour of a vaudeville style in the first act and structurally I needed to revisit this, (mirror) so these earlier scenes didn't just disappear as oddities (though oddities – wildcards, can also be good). In addition, using an old music-hall song would be a change from the heavier Schnittke, Mozart and Fred Frith material I'd been using in Act Two.

After the news of Lucy's death had been conveyed by the Lord showing Jonathan and Mina his bloody hands, I had Jonathan stand up, pulling focus. All the cast looks to him, and it is clear he is about to say something. But *we* don't need to hear what he says because we already know what happened. We only need to know that he is going to tell it to the others. I also don't need to show that he is telling them *how* to find the Count – I can show this by what they do next. So I froze that moment of eye contact between Jonathan and the others, had the lighting change to a flickering sepia film or postcard moment, and played Florrie Forde's version of 'Down at the Old Bull and Bush'. The carriage wheels from Act One were set at the back and turned, creating the image of a fairground and an old storybook. The lights cross faded as the three vampire brides dressed as street girls appeared holding a model of Dracula's house. The vampire brides drove a lot of *Dracula* like a Greek chorus (a traditional tried and tested structural method), and in this scene they lured the men across the stage, the men holding the obligatory flaming torches of a lynch mob, and leading them on into the squalid parts of town to find the creature Dracula, and the creature in themselves. Jonathan led the line, taking control of the situation – ah yes – this must be what he was about to tell them in that frozen moment. The men moved on a strict diagonal and each took turns looking over their shoulders as they went on into the dark – they could be looking about the seedy east end streets they were walking through, or looking back at who they were as they move forward towards what they are to become. At first the vampire brides acknowledged the audience, then they turned their attention to the men who did not. So the scene was ironic, humorous, symbolic and revisited a style of story telling introduced earlier in the production by reintroducing (repetition) the model of the house that had appeared in Act One. This scene gave the audience a little respite before the final third of the production.

I've mentioned wildcards before. I always ask if is there something else I could just drop into a production that is different, but somehow connected. Sometimes I find a wildcard that nudges in fine, and sometimes it doesn't work. That's fine, I chuck it in the bin. A wildcard dropped into a production that adds a new colour, a new perspective, can challenge my thought process.

There will come a time when you are sick and bored of your material. This is inevitable; if you are working and reworking things you can't expect that spark to be there all the time. Use this time as a positive. Don't think about being inspired, think about getting your head down and doing your job. It is sometimes easier to do this without yearning to being inspired all the time. It is the same as training to be a dancer. Be mechanical about it; clean and tighten things up. This is an essential part of the rehearsal process and dancers need this time. You have to dismantle everything, check and polish the components and put them together again, during which time there will be a period where it's not all working and you may feel things have got lost. Trust that all this diligent work will be apparent when you get a second wind and can re-spark the flame.

As you get further into your rehearsal period and your production is coming together you will have more people around you – the studio will be visited by managers, production managers, commissioners, producers, promoters, PR, marketing and others. Your ritual space will be invaded. What all these people will be seeing is unfinished – know that it is, and blank out what you *think* people might be thinking. They may be thinking good things, bad things, or just seeing where you are and not yet forming an opinion. Just keep going.

Some choreographers like to share their process early on. I don't. I don't want to show something that I know is not clear yet and be told it's not clear and advised on how to make it clear. I'll do that. I don't want people to try and work out what it is I'm trying to achieve when I'm in the middle of working this out myself. When I think something is getting there, forming a picture, then I might invite a few people whose opinions and perspective I respect to come and have a look to tell me what they see. I don't tend to seek out too many opinions, partly because it is *my* work, I know what I'm aiming for and am too busy just getting on with it all.

When should we listen, or not listen, to outside opinions? Whose opinions matter to you? Who do you trust? Who really understands your work? Who has the skill and the eye that means their opinions are constructive? Often it isn't the people with the loudest voices, or the ones most eager to voice their opinions. Consider the individual offering their opinion. Are they like you and your people, or are they from another world? If they are from another world, do they still get what you are about? What is their take on everything? This can be very interesting. It can also good for someone who doesn't know you to say what they see in the work. We do need input from others but there is no easy way to assess whether advice or a view of your work is right and you have to take each case as it comes. Sometimes an opinion from someone you don't really respect can open up another question within you, not perhaps what was intended.

I have at times over the course of my career been viciously attacked for what I do. If you worry too much about what other people say you won't have the confidence to make anything. The more productions you make the more you'll notice how many more self-appointed critics and gurus are out there than people actually making work. Do your best and see it through. I've had people completely pull my work apart just before it opens, only to see afterwards that their opinions were completely wrong; other times I've realised something someone said has been right, I just couldn't see it at the time. It's impossible to be sure you are right about everything, but it must be you that makes the decisions. Once your production is before an audience you are going to be bombarded by opinions. Every work I make could fall on its face. This is because I push myself beyond what I know every time I embark on a new project. Life is short – are you going to step into the unknown or play safe?

An example of when it *is* good to listen: I attended a workshop once in which we made material and shared it with each other. The mentor of the workshop had also been observing us work. He asked the group – 'where are you directing your dancers to look?' He brought this up because he'd heard me go on and on about eyeline – I kept lowering it, being very specific with the dancers. I was creating a kind of 'bull', something ready to charge. The mentor asked what people 'saw' as a result of this instruction. He said he saw 'avoidance'. This simple statement completely changed my work, and since then I have only asked dancers to look down if I have a very specific reason for doing so. I think it was a hang-up from my teenage years that was still there. These kinds of opinions are like gold: they can propel you forward years, and not just as an artist. The same happened to me many times as a dancer. A single personal correction can change your whole attitude towards how you move. I constantly reassess everything. Things get lodged so deeply in us we don't see they are there. They can get buried under other things, and finding the blockage that is preventing us from moving forward can be increasingly difficult – in many ways this gets harder as we get older, because we are swamped by the baggage we've collected on our journey.

Final drafts before tech

Y-ou have done a redraft. Another one. You have rehearsed and rehearsed, making sure everything is tight. Your dancers have grown in their parts; hopefully they are having a good time exploring them. You have all gone through the stage of being uninspired in what you are doing, but you are coming out of that now, reaping the rewards of your hard work. You are tired but you must do that final check, like when you sit an exam at school and are told to read through your work and check it one more time – you sit there thinking 'I can't be bothered, I'm sure it's alright', but if you do check you will always find some mistakes, and those mistakes cost you marks. Do the same here with your final studio time, when the lights are harsh and bright and things are not hidden or enhanced by the other elements that are soon to come into play. Choreography and character can be improved, but, better than that, you can make some final changes now that the work is rehearsed and before you (although you have been so close to it now you have to work at your objectivity). It is possible that one important decision can be made at this stage that will make your piece a hundred times better.

Know now that there will be all sorts of other distractions. Your rehearsal period will have been punctuated by production meetings and now all those details will be falling into place. You will be making constant decisions about set and costume before you begin tech. Any choices clear to you now, make them, so your team can be as prepared as possible before getting into the theatre, where they will have a million other things to deal with. Trust things are going on, that people are doing their jobs but double check anything you think you might not have been clear about. Don't expect to get a lunch break, (actually I've almost given up on lunch breaks these days – if you don't expect one then they seem like a bonus). And expect to be still sorting things well into the night and making decisions in your sleep. If you sleep.

Check the production schedule way in advance of production week. Make sure it is logical and everyone has the time they need. Don't call your dancers into the theatre until they need to be there. Having all these practical details to contend with can be a real hindrance to creative concentration but you just have to deal with this. Good management will try and keep things in check, but at the end of the day there are some questions that only you can answer. This is when having a good team really comes in to play; dealing with practicalities is one thing, but if you find yourself in the position of having to chase and remind them, then someone in your team isn't on the case.

I preempt what people are going to ask of me, because I don't want distractions at this time. I will have mulled over copy, images, poster and leaflet design well in advance. I will have kept an eye on everything that needs to go into the programme; from lists of music, right down to thank yous and whether to include character names on the cast list. It's surprising how long some of these things take to get right. I also appreciate that people are trying to do their jobs and I never want to delay things from my side. My advice is to always be ahead of the game.

Production week/tech

Tech is long hours, a lot of work to do as all elements of a production are brought together in a venue and put on the stage (in some cases it can include actually building a stage and lighting rig). Others need their time – production manager, stage manager, lighting, set, costume, sound; all logistics. You also need to schedule in a photo call for press and production shots. The last thing anyone needs is a director or choreographer who hasn't finished their job. (The truth is you won't have finished, but there is a difference between not having got your act together, and having everything in place so you have time to make final decisions about the production.) Something will always come up that you can't control, but I aim in the final rehearsal week to be running the production every day; everything that can be possibly worked out will have been and it will be practiced. We will know the venue we are going into and all exits and entrances will have been plotted, including where costume changes will take place (often this involves a difficult or nonexistent crossover, meaning at times your costume will be literally inaccessible). We won't waste tech time discovering things we have already found solutions for. We will have done full run-throughs with costume, make-up and set changes. It will be military. Once we get into the theatre space we will be ready to take on the added element – that all this is going to take place in the dark. And my pieces tend to be very dark. I don't know how the dancers find their way around.

Let your production team get on with it. Leave your lighting designer to it. It is usual to do a cue meeting before tech week (when all lighting, sound and music cues are confirmed with what is happening on stage; sometimes the cues are visual, sometimes timed). Often these cues have been established along the way, it is just a question of specifically honing them. Sometimes I don't even have a cue meeting because I trust that stage management and lighting will have it all down. People can get very stressed in techs, they can start shouting and losing it. This doesn't happen in my company. There is no need for a tech to be stressful if it has been planned properly. Problems will come up but there will be space to deal with them.

When the get-in, light rig, focus and plotting are done, work through the production scene by scene. Do this with stops, get everything clear and right. Then run scenes together with costume and set changes. Make adjustments and changes as you go. The days are long, there is a lot of hanging around. Do not expect your dancers to go full out in their dancing, just expect accuracy in timing and spacing. Don't waste energy thinking 'why isn't this working?' – be confident it is all there. Once you have got to the end of the piece, begin running it. During this time things will be ironed out, the bolts and screws tightened; the dancers will be going forward now; gearing up towards full performance with all the elements in play. This is now shaping up to be the rendition of your final production. Are there some decisions you want to make? If you have been organised with your tech you should have time to do this.

Listen to your instinct. Is there something in the work just waiting for you to set it free? When I made *Sea of Bones* originally only the cowgirls were painted blue. In tech, with full make-up something wasn't right – the world I wanted only seemed realised when the cowgirls appeared. I looked back to my original 'mind films' of how I'd envisaged this piece all that time ago, and realised in those films *everyone* was blue, but for one girl who gradually became this colour as she slipped into the world of the others. The piece was about the bones of our ancestry, the dead residing inside us, and about accepting and making peace with different sides of ourselves. From that moment on everyone painted themselves blue and things fell into place.

Often in dance you don't have previews like you do with theatre productions. Previews allow a production to grow on stage before a live audience. A show continues to grow in performance once it has officially opened, but a preview audience is open and interested in a production still undergoing a creative process, changing and finding its feet. With dance you are often opening your show in one of your main venues and the press is there. I advocate previews, and so I run this side of things more like a theatre production.

First night

Something that began life as a handful of ideas a long time ago has become this production before you. You won't really know what you have created until later. Making productions have become markers, chapters in my life that I can look back on, and because of them I can more easily remember who I was at a particular time, and in hindsight often understand myself better than at the actual time.

Don't be surprised at feeling a little numb when the audience is coming into the theatre. At this time something in me steps back, I tend to think of my life and wonder again at what I do – what a way to earn a living – and something in me kind of laughs. I don't tend to get nervous, I get philosophical. There is nothing I can do now.

The pressures of creating work can affect your health at times, but you can work at having a healthy attitude. When you are young you have more energy, and you can make mistakes, you can lose a year here or there, you have fewer responsibilities – children, a mortgage, all these adult things that happen when you realise that life isn't a game, and that you are actually walking a tightrope. The older we get the more we realise how big the world is, and how little we know. I didn't dwell on failure too much when I was young – I was so obsessed with trying to express myself I didn't worry about consequences or getting things wrong. I'm more experienced and considered now, less self-obsessed, but I continue to maintain a singleminded determination to create work. You learn from experience. Be bold, don't creep forward if you have a strong vision. Don't let fear rule you

List of stills